What people are saying about *The Beautiful Ache*

"*The Beautiful Ache* is a rare jewel that helps us to better understand the deep longings of our hearts—and to know that amidst the disappointments and struggles of this life, there is yet a joy and hope so powerful and so real that it transforms even the most ordinary of lives."

Frank Reich, pastor, Cornerstone Presbyterian Church,
Charlotte, NC

"I so resonate with Leigh's descriptions about a little-understood longing in our hearts. Surely this book will help others identify their own longings . . . and the only Source that satisfies."

Carol Kuykendall, MOPS International

"If you want to play it safe, swaddle yourself in comfort, or wall off your heart beyond pain's reach, don't read *The Beautiful Ache*. Leigh McLeroy, a master storyteller, beckons readers to risk suffering and failure in order to experience real joy. *The Beautiful Ache* is an awakening to Jesus in all of life, an invitation that we take hold of the life that is truly LIFE."

Glenn Lucke, president of Docent Research Group and
coauthor of *Common Grounds:*
Conversations about Things That Matter Most

"Leigh is a careful thinker with a deep grasp of God's Word who has the rare ability to translate her insight into prose that sings, dances, and remains fixed in the reader's memory."

Steve Halliday, president, Crown Media Ltd., Portland, OR

"In *The Beautiful Ache*, Leigh McLeroy holds my hand in a place I know, but that I fear. With honesty and hope, she leads me to lean into the longing and find joy on the other side. Her fearlessness has become my courage, and I am eternally grateful. Thank you, Leigh, for your companionship in the journey."

Judy Nelson, editor-in-chief, *Worldwide Challenge* magazine, Orlando, FL

"*The Beautiful Ache* is a well-written reminder of why we are really here and where many of us are headed. The book is a heavenly read."

Steve Arterburn, author and host of New Life Live radio, Newport Beach, CA

"This book challenges readers in a poetic and even prophetic way to join the wild and wonderful adventure of following Christ in the ordinary moments of our lives. Leigh McLeroy has skillfully and deftly woven the grace and beauty of the gospel into a wonderful tapestry of stories."

Ben Young, pastor and author, Houston, TX

THE
Beautiful
ACHE

FINDING *the* GOD WHO SATISFIES
WHEN LIFE DOES NOT

LEIGH McLEROY

Revell
Grand Rapids, Michigan

© 2007 by Leigh McLeroy

Published by Fleming H. Revell
a division of Baker Publishing Group
P.O. Box 6287, Grand Rapids, MI 49516-6287

Printed in the United States of America

Library of Congress Cataloging-in-Publication Data
McLeroy, Leigh.
    The beautiful ache : finding the God who satisfies when life does not / Leigh McLeroy.
      p. cm.
    Includes bibliographical references.
    ISBN 10: 0-8007-3141-7 (pbk.)
    ISBN 978-0-8007-3141-0 (pbk.)
    1. Spirituality. 2. Consolation. I. Title.
    BV4501.3.M373 2007
    248.4—dc22   2006027914

Published in association with the literary agency of Alive Communications, Inc., 7680 Goddard Street, Suite 200, Colorado Springs, CO 80920.

Godspeed, Leighton. And thank you.

Contents

Foreword   9
Acknowledgments   11
Prologue   13

1. Are We There Yet?   15
   The Ache of Traveling
2. Watching the Horse Whisperer   29
   The Ache to Belong
3. Beautiful Joe   43
   The Ache of Persevering
4. One Golden Dancing Shoe   57
   The Ache to Celebrate
5. The Front Porch Castaway   71
   The Ache for Adventure
6. "Have Courage"   85
   The Ache to Hear God
7. One Bright Red Bird   99
   The Ache of Hope
8. Faith and Falling   111
   The Ache of Trusting
9. "Gimme Some Sugar"   125
   The Ache for Healing

10. Scrabble in Stocking Feet   139
    The Ache of Expecting
11. New Clothes for Cara   153
    The Ache for Beauty
12. Old Addresses   165
    The Ache of Memory
13. "You're Fired!"   179
    The Ache of Labor
14. Lost Causes   193
    The Ache of a Prodigal
15. Goodbye, Rhett Butler   207
    The Ache of Grief
16. Singing the Hymnal   221
    The Ache to Worship
17. A Table in the Wilderness   235
    The Ache to Feast with God

    Epilogue   247
    Notes   249

Foreword

I'm not big on surveys, but one in particular stands out in my mind—even though it's been twenty years since I first heard of it. According to sociologist Anthony Campolo, a survey was taken of a hundred people one hundred years of age and older who were asked this one simple question: "If you had to live your life over again, what would you do differently?" Though a variety of answers were offered, the majority of the centenarians surveyed said this: First, we would risk more. Second, we would reflect more. Third, we would focus on things that make a lasting impact.

Risk.

Reflect.

Make a lasting impact.

I love that survey. In a world that values safety over risk, efficiency over reflection, and the immediate over the eternal, these wise sages' simple yet profound words challenge me deeply.

As I read *The Beautiful Ache*, my heart pounded with this threefold desire to risk more, reflect more, and focus on things that will have a lasting impact. This book challenges readers in a poetic and even prophetic way to join the wild and wonderful adventure of following Christ in the ordinary moments of our lives. Leigh McLeroy has skillfully and deftly woven the grace and beauty of the gospel into a wonderful tapestry of stories.

The more I read the book, the more I wanted to keep reading it. I almost finished it in one sitting. The chapters became addictive, and the stories were like a good, suspenseful movie that leaves you wondering, "Who dunnit?" until the last scene. Throughout the pages, I could hear the echoes of the centenarians calling and wooing us all to risk, reflect, and focus on things that will last forever.

But make no mistake, *The Beautiful Ache* is not a feel-good, Christianity-lite, chicken-broth-for-the-shallow-soul read. Though you will feel inspired, warm, and satisfied when reading this book, it's fashioned in a way that does not sacrifice truth on the altar of sentimentality. Leigh deals with the deep issues of lifelike suffering, death, and disappointment—in a realistic, yet hopeful way. She winsomely calls us to embrace beauty and pain, justice and mercy, and work and play by showing how the gospel plays out in all of these areas. Few writers possess the ability to tackle these tough and complex subjects with such compassion and insight.

I have no doubt you will enjoy the book you hold in your hand. Go grab a cup of coffee and a bagel. Turn off your cell phone and Crackberry. Find a comfortable chair and read away. You will feel and hear the beautiful ache deep inside, and be gracefully ignited to follow the One who truly satisfies the longing of your soul.

Ben Young, pastor and author
Houston, Texas

Acknowledgments

*M*y family was my first reading audience, and they've applauded every single effort, even the ones that probably didn't merit much enthusiasm. They believed in me. They still do. So Dad, Mom, Lynn—here's another try at truth. I hope it rings truest for you. Katharine and Victoria: If you can learn anything at all from my mistakes, do. You two have made my life so bright, and I love you as if you were my own.

To the precious friends who've read and reread these words many times over—thank you. Your wisdom informs mine, and your love steadies me. I am blessed.

Leighton Ogg, thank you for helping me find my voice, and for telling me about the horse whisperer. See what you started?

Lee Hough, you championed this project, pressed for clarity, and made even the "no's" seem encouraging. You're amazing. I am grateful. Let's do it again.

Jeanette Thomason, breakfast with you in Denver was like a breath of fresh air. Thanks for pushing for a "yes." Jennifer Leep, you made the transition seamless. Working with you and your colleagues at Revell has been a pleasure, plain and simple.

And to the One who is first and last, beginning and end, best and brightest . . . Jesus, I love you. I am yours.

Prologue

*I*t's the pang that strikes when loss is sudden, or suddenly realized. It's the stealthy tears that fall when something stunningly grand (or nakedly simple) sets holiness on clear display. It arrives with crickets chirping on a June night, or a bright pink sunset slung low and wide across the sky, or the sound of a child's sleepy whisper. It lingers in memory-infused music and nibbles the edges of silent hope. It's evoked by a longed-for touch or a word well spoken, delivered just in time. It invades carpool lines and conference rooms with equal deftness. It is no respecter of place or time.

It's the beautiful ache. It says, *There's more.*

More than you've seen and much more than you've longed for. Beyond what you know and far, far past your strongest yearning. As C. S. Lewis said, "If I find in myself a desire which no experience in this world can satisfy, the most probable explanation is that I was made for another world."[1]

The beautiful ache is that fleeting pang that reminds us of home. Not the home we've always known—the home we've never seen. The ache pierces and pries open the heart but doesn't nearly satisfy it. It whets the appetite but doesn't begin to fill it.

It unmasks beauty but not completely. It reeks of truth but stops just short of telling all.

Hardly a day goes by that I don't feel it. The trick is learning to allow the ache to take me where it wants to go, to tutor and tantalize my mostly numb senses with its laser-sharp aim. The challenge is to not kill it off before it fully arrives or dismiss it before it is ready to go.

I don't have to ask if you know what I'm talking about. You do. You've felt the ache too.

So what if the next time it came you opened your heart just a little wider and allowed it even further in? What if you offered the ache a standing invitation to visit whenever it liked, to drop in anytime it was "in the neighborhood"? What if you denied the urge to fill the crevice or crater-like space it makes with activity or noise or food or drink—and simply sat with it awhile?

Could you learn to love such wide-awake living? Could you joyfully taste heaven one exquisite morsel at a time without feeling the need to either push the smallish plate away or lick it clean, demanding more?

Somewhere a sick child struggles to celebrate a birthday that could be his last. A dogwood tree blooms in April. An ivory china-plate moon hangs low in the October sky. A dear friend dies. A baby laughs. Two lovers make impossible vows and mean to keep them. A soldier sends his love home, wishing he could deliver it in person. An old hymn is sung. A new book is written. A familiar tale is retold, growing richer with the telling.

The beautiful ache points us beyond. It is not meant to be ignored. So when it comes—and it will—why not move in closer and ask the ache what true and terrible secrets it knows and longs to tell? You won't regret it.

> "But our citizenship is in heaven. And we eagerly await a Savior from there, the Lord Jesus Christ" (Phil. 3:20 NIV).

Are We There Yet?

The Ache of Traveling

O send out Your light and Your truth, let them bring me;
Let them bring me to Your holy hill,
And to Your dwelling places.

Psalm 43:3

In between one place and another, we're vulnerable to the discomfort of our transitory state. If the trip is long or taxing, at odd mile markers our restlessness overrides expectation, or even drifts into despair. When trouble comes we may wonder why we ever embarked at all—or simply stop short of our intended destination, insisting (like the Israelites east of Jordan) that the spot we've settled for is adequate enough, thank you. The best of all journeys may be a hard road to a good place; perhaps fully experiencing the hard, unpredictable road helps us to recognize the good place when we arrive.

*E*very parent who's ever breathed has no doubt heard the cry that every child in transit has uttered: "Are we *there* yet?" Sometimes the words are repeated in chattering expectation; sometimes they are sighed in resigned weariness. But regardless of their tone or frequency, their prompting is the same: the longing to be somewhere we are not. For those of us who are no longer children, the stakes of our grown-up journey are much higher than we may admit. Our hoped-for destination is not Disneyland or grandmother's house or a favorite campsite. We are not traveling in a loaded station wagon with a Styrofoam ice chest in the back. This journey is just as real—but our destination is a true kingdom, not a magic one. And our goal is not simply transport or amusement. *It is abundant, vibrant, God-glorifying, soul-satisfying life.*

The mystery of our anticipated kingdom lies in the fact that it is both present and future, now and not yet. It overlaps the edges and sometimes intersects the very heart of this ragged world—but it comes from another place altogether. In those overlapping, intersecting moments, our desire is most keenly felt. We *know* we're made for more than this. We're just not sure whether to bury our longings or embrace them—whether to deny the disappointments of everyday life or dive deeper and plumb their depths. Like it or not, we live each day struggling to reconcile "how it is" with "how we hoped it would be."

And the ache persists. Money can't make it go away, and love can't quench it entirely. It won't be wrestled into submission by activity or power or subterfuge. C. S. Lewis once said that if we

17

find in ourselves a desire which no earthly thing can satisfy, the logical conclusion must be that we are made for another world. And so we are.

Blow-dried meteorologists invoked their grim mantra over and over as I sat before the television, trying to absorb the reality of what a category five storm might mean to my sprawling Gulf Coast city. "Run from water," the weather gurus repeated, "hide from wind." Friends called to confer: "Are you leaving? Where are you going? When will you go?" We discussed things that had never before come up in the course of conversation, like whether or not we lived in the one-hundred-year floodplain (half of Houston does) and what records or belongings we ought to take with us, should we decide to evacuate.

I called my sister and brother-in-law. They were staying close to care for his elderly parents. I called my parents. Staying, in a split vote. I had a ready refuge two hundred miles north, and my family encouraged me to go. A good friend had offered her home so that I could at least work and not risk being without power for several days. I could even bring my dog, she said, knowing full well I wouldn't have left without him. I wavered for a full day as the storm grew, gaining speed and intensity, but after hearing a host of elected officials urge everyone who could travel to do so, I decided to head north. Run from water, hide from wind, they said. I set my alarm for 4:30 and went to bed. I was going to run before sunrise.

My ringing cell phone awakened me at 5:45. The alarm had failed to go off, but the car was loaded—and after hearing my dad's last-minute instructions (take plenty of water; be sure you have a full tank of gas; be very careful; call often to let me know where you are), I put my dog Chester in the seat beside me and our northward exodus began. I thought the four-and-a-half-hour trip might take me as much as twelve hours, and I had prepared myself for that. But nothing could have prepared me for the eighteen-hour purgatory that would soon unfold.

Less than a half mile from my home, the freeway shut down to a crawl. An accident was blocking the three right lanes, the radio informed me. I dutifully merged left and waited. Forty-five minutes later, I was sailing north, but my burst of speed didn't last long. I had traveled only another handful of miles before coming to a literal halt on the interstate. Ahead of me as far as I could see was a line of brake lights. I turned the radio up and heard the bad news: gridlock for a hundred miles, with over a million people (and me) traveling out of the city toward safety. It was, quite literally, an exodus of biblical proportions.

I took a quick inventory. I had a quart or more of water. Dry cereal and some juice packets. A full tank of gas. A cell phone and charger. But it wasn't yet 7:00 a.m., and already I could feel the heat rising from the asphalt beneath me. The radio announcer said to expect temperatures nearing 100 degrees throughout the day, and I knew that sitting in a running car with the air conditioner blowing would use up precious fuel. Being hot was far better than being stranded, I reasoned. I would use the air conditioner sparingly, only when I needed to cool us down. I rolled down the windows and turned off the engine. The uncertain wait was on.

Cars were parked for miles on the freeway. People got out and walked from one car to the next, talking to strangers as if they were neighbors. The couple in front of me was from Maryland, trying to catch a flight out of the airport some twenty miles away. They offered me pistachios and chatted good-naturedly as we waited to inch forward another few yards. I prayed they would make their flight and get home. I prayed I would make my destination too, but the signs were not encouraging. Not at all. Four and a half hours later, I was approaching the airport.

On a normal day, the same trip would have taken me twenty-five minutes or less. The heat was becoming unbearable. Chester was panting, but he refused to drink. I began wetting the top of his head with water, fearful that my decision to leave would cause this to be the last trip we would take together.

My radio DJ wingman offered no encouragement at all. He reported that every artery out of town was essentially shut down and not moving. Department of transportation engineers were devising ways to make all incoming lanes outgoing—a massive contra-flow plan that included every freeway but the one I was on. Then he not-so-judiciously announced that a family of four had just called in to say that their family pet had expired in the car. I cried for the first time.

If I could have turned around then, I would have. Movement, even in the wrong direction, was preferable to being trapped in the heat and having my dog die in my lap. But there was simply no way to reverse the path that I had chosen. I was on a course that could not be changed—at least not anytime soon. Every hour or so, when I could get a cell tower signal, I spoke with my dad. He offered alternate routes if and when I could exit the interstate. My sister did likewise. Ultimately I would use one of those routes, but not for several more hours. The familiar voices of my family became my lifeline. I needed to believe that someone knew my whereabouts. I needed them to tell me I would be okay. I tried to keep my voice from sounding frightened as we spoke, but I could not begin to mask its weariness. I was bone tired, sweating, and stroking the head of the limp and panting dog draped across my lap. Every time I wet his head, the words "I baptize thee" came strangely and soundlessly to mind. I prayed the water would soothe him, even if he would not drink. I sipped from a juice pack, but not often, since bathroom breaks were a complete impossibility. And we waited in mind-numbing limbo for something ahead of us to move.

Like me, the Israelites were barely "out of town" before their massive and miraculous exodus screeched to a halt. Backed into a corner at the edge of the Red Sea, they faced the sure menace of Pharaoh's oncoming army. The only choice left to them seemed to be not *whether* to die but *how*: by an Egyptian soldier's sword, or by slow drowning in salty waves? The same God who—by plagues and miracles—had weakened Pharaoh's resolve to keep Israel in slavery now changed the Egyptian ruler's heart again: "For Pharaoh will say of the sons of Israel, 'They are wandering aimlessly in the land; the wilderness has shut them in.' Thus I will harden Pharaoh's heart, and he will chase after them; and I will be honored through Pharaoh and all his army, and the Egyptians will know that I am the LORD" (Exod. 14:3–4).

It made no sense. Why would God lead his people out and then threaten their very lives? Why would he arrange the all-too-soon showdown at the Red Sea? For his own glory, the Bible records. For his renown. For his great fame and name. It seems that more was at stake than the Israelites' straight, comfortable, and expeditious journey to the promised richness of Canaan. Their going out was as much about the trip itself as it was the destination. They may have been focused simply on getting from point A to point B. God was focused on much, much more than that. Through time and tears and hardship, he would build their faith and cause them to boast in his provision. He would make believers out of opposing armies and prove his faithfulness again and again. His chosen ones were weak and dependent. He was mighty and strong. This was the truth they would be called to relearn at every bend in the road.

Were they pleased with the painful and unpredictable nature of their God-led journey? No, they were not. They grumbled. They railed at Moses. They reinvented for themselves a happy

21

history in Egypt, where in fact they had been miserable slaves. They even questioned whether it had been necessary to embark at all if death was to be their certain end: "Then they said to Moses, 'Is it because there were no graves in Egypt that you have taken us away to die in the wilderness? Why have you dealt with us in this way, bringing us out of Egypt?'" (Exod. 14:11).

But the Red Sea did not prove to be the scene of their demise. Anyone who's seen Cecil B. DeMille's *The Ten Commandments* knows how the showdown ended: God instructed Moses to send the Israelites into the water and to lift his staff over the sea and divide it. (I try to imagine how implausible these instructions must have sounded to Moses; I simply cannot.) God ordered—and Moses obeyed. The Egyptians gave chase, but the wall of water that protected God's people did not stand for their enemies. The Egyptians drove their chariots and armies into the sea in chase, and chaos ensued. Then Moses lifted his staff again and the waiting waters gave way, drowning the chariots, the horsemen, and Pharaoh's entire army.

Could unarmed Israel have defeated Egypt in their own strength if they had turned and fought at the edge of the sea? Not likely. Had a single Israelite ever witnessed a body of water—*any* body of water—cleave itself in two? Negative again. But these end-result-oriented people were only just getting to know their process-happy God. In the months and years that ensued, they would find themselves helpless and held fast by circumstance many times, and he would surprise them at every turn.

He led them to twelve springs of water in Elim when they thought they would die of thirst. But he didn't quench their thirst that same way again. The next time he brought water from a rock instead. He fed them with strange stuff from heaven called manna, but just enough for each day. Its properties were oddly fleeting, and it could not be stored up in advance. They were forced to gather it anew each morning, and each morning he provided more. He gave them bread at sunrise and meat at sunset. He led them with a cloud by day and a column of fire by night. He routed armies before them and confounded their enemies. They grew in faith, and he got glory. Lots of it. But they would never have chosen such a rigorous drill had the choice been left to them. They were learning to be God's people in God's presence by God's power. They were tasting his kingdom, still miles and years from Canaan.

As traffic crept along the interstate at a snail's pace, I eyed the gas gauge. It had dropped below half a tank, and I was still hours from my destination. My friend called and suggested an alternate plan if I could not get to her home by nightfall. Her former college roommate lived an hour or two closer and would be glad to take me in. If I could not get to her, she and her husband would come for me, wherever I was en route. "Get as far as you possibly can," she said. "Don't stop. Help is coming."

I exited the interstate onto a farm road that would carry me north and west, then crawled along on it for twenty miles. (Others, it seemed, had had the same idea.) At least this road was shaded by tall pine trees, and the heat was less intense. I rolled down the windows and felt a slight breeze. Chester turned his face into the wind. I was grateful for such a small but welcomed grace, and I whispered heartfelt thanks. Haltingly, start and stop, start and stop, I made my way to another interstate—this one turned into a six-lane contra-flow, heading north. Moving on it at more than ten miles per hour felt like driving the autobahn. I spoke with my dad again. "As soon as you can, start looking for gas," he urged. I *had* been looking, but every station I'd passed had either shuttered up entirely or placed white plastic bags over the pump handles to show they had already sold what little gas they had.

Finally, with less than a third of a tank left, I spotted an open station with a long line of cars. I pulled in behind the last one and prepared to wait another hour or more for fuel, praying the supply would not run out before my turn came. I thought of the God who provided oil for the Maccabees and bread for the multitudes and prayed that he would provide fossil fuel for me. I put Chester on his leash, gave him water and a few bites of kibble, and let him explore. I carried him inside with me for a break and then returned to my car to inch toward the pumps.

In front of me, a man in a Michael Jordan T-shirt smiled. I smiled back. When his turn came to pump, I stepped out of the car again. "Where are you coming from?" he asked.

"Houston," I said.

"Where are you headed?"

"Tyler tonight, I hope," I said. "How about you?"

"Got family in Crockett," he replied. "I think we'll stop there." Then he eyed my car and my now energized four-legged traveling companion. "Is that your posse?" he asked.

"That would be it," I nodded.

"Come on now," he teased. "Where's that man of yours?"

"Don't know. I guess he hasn't found me yet," I said.

He smiled again. "How about a thirteen-year-old ball player? I coach a boys' basketball team back home."

The line got a chuckle. I think that was his intent. We wished one another a safe journey, and then he and his family were off.

I had enough gas now to reach my final destination, but traffic and time would not cooperate. I continued to inch forward until darkness fell. It felt much, much lonelier in the dark, but at least it was cool. I spoke with my friend's former roommate, who assured me I had a place for the night. Then she called twice more to check my progress and encourage me. I hadn't eaten all day, and my eyelids were getting heavy. Chester had finally fallen asleep. My dad called every hour or so to ask where I was, far past the time he would have normally been in bed. When I finally reached the turnoff to Crockett, a familiar-looking SUV pulled up beside me, and in the red glow I saw its driver smile and wave. It was my gas line friend. He had followed me for the last fifty miles, but I hadn't known.

With less than another fifty miles to go, I was able to drive the speed limit for the first time since morning. I turned on the radio, searching for a station that would come in clearly, and stopped when I heard a familiar pastor's soothing voice. I was smack in the middle of the Bible Belt, where gospel preachers compete with rock stars and country crooners for AM airtime. I listened as this one began to recite the beautiful words of Psalm 23. I whispered them out loud with him. God was providing for me on my run from the storm, just as he had for his people on the run from Pharaoh. Run from water, hide from wind. Run from water, hide from wind. And run *into* the arms of the shepherd whose name is Jesus. The weathermen hadn't said that hours ago, but they should have.

I don't know how many times in my childhood I asked, "Are we there yet?" Too many to count, I am sure. I do remember the urgent desire, even when comfortably settled in the back of my parents' car with a book or a pad of paper or a doll, to be somewhere *other* than where I was. I longed for those places I knew and had visited before—familiar, much-loved destinations where hugs and smiles and adventure surely waited. In a short time I wanted the trips to be over and done so the destination could be seen and enjoyed. It was always either/or back then. Never both/and.

But it's different today. Today I am painfully aware that I belong to another world—one I haven't seen and can only imagine.

I live en route, in between. And as much as I dream of heaven, I love this life on earth. I love the sights and sounds and smells of it, the faces of family and friends, and the comforts of music and art and laughter and delicious meals. I love worship and travel and a warm cup of coffee between my hands, and seasons and solitude and sleeping dogs. Still, I yearn for what I haven't gained but have only glimpsed. I long for more than the simple goodnesses I have known.

Because I believe that more exists, this life is my exodus, not my end. Because the way itself is rich, I want to travel it with purpose, passion, and as much joy as I can muster. I know the ache of long miles slowly paced, and of heat and fear and loneliness. I know that on the journey hearts break and storms come and plans change (oh, how they change!). But thankfully, on the way to the Good, the True, and the Beautiful, we encounter the good, the true, and the beautiful—even as we travel with the unpleasant companions of disappointment, pain, and despair. The secret of savoring the journey into the fullness of the kingdom is to refuse to either kill our present desire *or* deny our dissatisfaction. The challenge is to live in the "now," fully engaged by its conflicts—and to long just as expectantly for that not-yet day when we will finally, breathlessly, completely arrive.

I didn't realize how good I had it years ago, traveling in the back of the family station wagon with my Barbies, books, and games. I was never asked to drive, the map was someone else's responsibility, the snacks were plentiful, and all roads led to adventure, then home. Journeying requires more of me these days—sometimes more than I feel I have to give. And I believe God means for it to.

Are you road-weary? Disillusioned? Have you settled in a place you never meant to linger for more than even an hour? Do you believe joy, comfort, and satisfaction are always "out there," just beyond the horizon? What if hints of your desired destination were very near and it really was possible to experience them, now, today?

"Who is like You among the gods, O LORD? Who is like You, majestic in holiness, awesome in praises, working wonders? . . . In Your lovingkindness You have led the people whom You have redeemed; in Your strength You have guided them to Your holy habitation. . . . You will bring them and plant them in the mountain of Your inheritance, the place, O LORD, which You have made for Your dwelling, the sanctuary, O LORD, which Your hands have established. The LORD shall reign forever and ever" (Exod. 15:11, 13, 17–18).

"You will make known to me the path of life; in Your presence is fullness of joy; in Your right hand there are pleasures forever" (Ps. 16:11).

"One thing I have asked from the LORD, that I shall seek: That I may dwell in the house of the LORD all the days of my life, to behold the beauty of the LORD and to meditate in His temple. For in the day of trouble He will conceal me in His tabernacle; in the secret place of His tent He will hide me; He will lift me up on a rock" (Ps. 27:4–5).

Watching the Horse Whisperer

The Ache to Belong

Truer words were never spoken
and to an audience of one
Where you're healed is where you're broken
God knows your native tongue.

David Wilcox, "Native Tongue"

I wouldn't have made it far in this following-Jesus life if I had doubted that I belonged to the One whose voice first called my name. I'm as sure of it as I have ever been of anything—and I've at least appeared sure of quite a lot. I'm still awed by the mystery that the God of the universe called me by name. When I need to know that I belong, I remember that call and how perfectly true it felt to be beckoned and to fall in behind his lead.

*I*f most little girls love horses, then I adored them. I might have grown up in the fourth-largest city in the United States, but in my heart I was a fresh-air-fed, free-spirited child of the great outdoors. Before boys became interesting, horses were my fiercest passion. I drew them with charcoal pencils. I painted them in oils. One summer I learned to decoupage, and my prize effort was a deckle-edged, heavily glazed print of a mare and foal standing side by side on a harvest gold, pressboard prairie. It hung in my bedroom all through high school, and I wish I had it now.

Horses spoke to this child's heart. I longed to win the affection of one, and I believed that given the chance, I could. So I begged for a horse. I didn't think it was likely that my parents would give in to my pleading, but I didn't relent for a long time.

One Christmas I believed with as much belief as a child can muster that there was a saddle in the trunk of my mother's car. There was something there—no doubt about it—and it seemed to me that the time was right for it to be a saddle. While the real thing never came along, my parents honored my desire with plenty of tokens that said they heard. Horse books and horse figurines crowded my tiny room. Some were plastic, some were polished ceramic—but all, to my eyes, were beautiful. I let them graze in the bookcase headboard of my narrow twin bed, in a polished maple pasture with a carved spindle fence.

My dream was growing smaller and more easily contained.

Soon enough my horses were packed away, replaced by photographs and dried corsages and books of poetry—things that gave little hint that an imaginary cowgirl had once laid her head nearby. I rode occasionally, but never a horse that was mine. I came close to forgetting the imagined bliss of running my hands over the satiny flank of a friend bigger than me, and I let go the thought of speaking a wordless language and being understood. I grew up. I put away childish things.

Then I read a novel about a horse whisperer. He saved a little girl's horse, and her horse saved her. (The grown-ups in the story fared less well.) This whisperer knew things, but he was in no hurry to prove them. A few years later, Hollywood produced a screenplay of the book, and the horse whisperer from its pages was fleshed out on celluloid by an aging Robert Redford. I saw the film version of the story. Twice. Then I bought my own copy on video. And years beyond my own horse-fancying days, on more than a few rainy afternoons or lonely evenings, I put this movie in the VCR and wept.

In my secret heart I was still a little horse-crazy, but no one else knew. I kept to my older, wiser self about it.

"Monty Roberts: The Man Who Listens to Horses," the photocopied flyer read. A friend had offered it with the casual suggestion that I might value an evening spent watching a real-life horse whisperer. Since I'd never expressed to him an interest in horses, I assumed there must be more behind the recommended program than a how-to demonstration on breaking a wild mustang—a skill I was not likely to require soon. This was a friend with a way of coming at truth on the slant, and that knowledge, along with my early enchantment with horses, was enough to get me out to the arena solo on a hazy, warm November night.

I pulled into the parking area of the equestrian center a good half hour before "showtime," and already the lot was nearly full. Pickup trucks outnumbered sedans ten to one, and boots, hats, and jeans were the unofficial uniform. Loosely packed pea gravel scrunched under my city-girl shoes as I made my way toward the lights of the arena. I could hear music playing in the distance—smooth, instrumental versions of western classics like "Don't Fence Me In" and "Tumbling Tumbleweeds." At the gate I handed over my ticket (a pricey twenty-five dollars, but with proceeds benefiting a state school for disabled children) and moved inside to find myself a seat in the bleachers.

A good twenty yards away, in the center of the arena floor, a circular pen was set up, and couples, teenagers, and middle-aged cowboy-types milled around it, looking at exhibits on horse trailers, veterinary information, and equine nutrition. I stayed put and people-watched, drinking in the view—a parallel universe to the office buildings, shopping malls, and suit-clad workers more familiar to me. I wondered where these folks lived and what kind of work they did. I wondered if they had any better idea than I of what they were about to see.

At seven thirty, after a few announcements, two men and a woman briskly walked into the arena. The woman, Pat Roberts, said a few words of welcome, then introduced her son Marty, who in turn introduced his father, Monty. The horse whisperer entered the pen to polite applause and began to walk and talk, explaining how he'd come to love and learn from the animal he called *Equus* and how he developed over time his gentle and remarkably successful method of training.

Monty Roberts was well into his sixties and looked it. He was a bulky, handsome man, and his words came out in short, breathy phrases, punctuated like a weekend jogger's running conversation. He would work with four horses that night, and he had never seen or touched any of them before. Their owners, present in the crowd, all verified this. An assistant brought the first horse into the ring, a seven-year-old paint named Little Willy. (Days later I laughed when I remembered the lyrics that surely must have inspired his name: "Little Willy-Willy won't go home, but you can't push Willy where Willy won't go . . .") According to Willy's owner, he'd never once been bridled, saddled, or ridden. He looked like the trouble his name implied.

After a brief "introduction" at the center of the pen, the horse whisperer squared up to face the paint and looked him directly in the eyes. Willy instantly perceived this as a threatening move and broke for the edge of the ring in a staccato scuffle of hooves. As Willy ran the fence, Monty talked. Horses, he explained, are flight animals. They've survived for who-knows-how-many years because of their ability to identify their predators and outrun them.

His voice was low, and its cadence was soothing and unhurried. As he continued to speak, Willy slowed up a bit and eased off the fence. A horse will only flee so far, Monty said. He will not run until he's exhausted. He'll go just far enough to get a safe perspective. Willy was instinctively trying to determine whether or not Monty was dangerous, whether he intended to harm or befriend.

"Now I'm looking for four things," Monty explained. "Willy will use these four things to tell me in his language that he's ready to negotiate." The first sign was that the horse would cock the ear closest to Monty inward at a forty-five-degree angle. In the language of *Equus*, this micromovement would say, "You have my attention. I'm focused and I'm listening." As Monty said this, almost on cue, Willy's inside ear turned toward the horse whisperer.

Next the horse would leave the perimeter of the pen and move in closer to the center, where Monty stood. And again, Willy mirrored the movement just described. At this point there was barely a sound except Willy's anxious snorts as he stepped toward this curious man. But instead of turning slightly away in order to reassure Willy that his approach was safe, Monty abruptly squared off on the horse again, sending him back to the perimeter. There was nothing tentative about his movement. "If you're going to send him away," he said, "don't send him away a little—send him away a lot." And he did.

The third gesture the trainer anticipated seemed particularly odd. The horse, Monty explained, would begin to lick and chew, moving his mouth in a way that mimicked eating or drinking. This would demonstrate that Willy did not fear the handler and believed he would not be hurt. (After all, you don't typically share a meal with an enemy.) I watched with total amazement as Willy's mouth began to move, as if to chew.

The fourth and last gesture Willy would offer was to lower his head close to the ground, allowing it to bob as he moved along. This action, according to Monty, was akin to the horse saying, "If we could have a meeting to renegotiate, I would let you be the chairman."

With all four gestures now demonstrated, the horse whisperer invited the horse to approach him again by looking away and turning his body at an angle to Willy's. What a human might perceive as a mixed message, Willy must have seen as an irresistible invitation. He moved in quietly behind Monty's shoulder, his nose almost pressed to the place where arm and torso are joined. Monty was still for a moment, then turned slightly and reached out with a soft, curved hand to stroke Willy's forehead, just between his eyes.

After a quick rub, he stepped away, and Willy, now seemingly more cocker spaniel than unbroken outlaw, followed him. As Monty moved around the pen, Willy moved with him. Every now and again, the whisperer reached up to stroke the horse's face and then stepped away. Each time, Willy followed like a house pet. This, Monty explained, was the moment of joining up.

This, I thought, was something altogether lovely.

As I watched, my throat became tight and dry. I swallowed hard and glanced to my right and left to see if anyone had noticed the slightly embarrassed, emotional woman nearby—the citified one who'd never owned a saddle or a horse. They hadn't. Their eyes were fixed on the ring. Something big had happened here. We had been given text and subtext. A story had unfolded before us with all its integral parts: antagonist, protagonist, conflict, climax, resolution.

Watching the horse whisperer that night, I began to understand something of the "horse thing" that has lodged in my heart since childhood. I say "began" because the whole meaning of the metaphor is not yet known to me. But now at least I knew that in my imagination, I had been miscast for years. I had seen *myself* as the whisperer—the one who would woo and charm and love the horse. And I suppose I might have. But what I really longed to be was the wooed one. The trusting one. The charmed and loved one who, for the right sort of invitation, would gladly stop running and let herself be led.

The relationship I watched being birthed that night between the horse and the man who beckoned him was not forced or coerced. It was carefully drawn and executed. Willy was chosen. Then Willy chose. The responder needed the initiator, even though he feared him at first. The initiator gave the responder full freedom to run—and more than once he did run. But after he ran as long as he needed to run, he came home and placed his face against the shoulder of the one who'd both called him and sent him away. And that moment—that lovely joining up—wasn't the end, it was the beginning.

Within thirty minutes, Willy would accept a blanket, bridle, saddle, and rider. But what would he do another day, in another ring or outside it? Would he remember and trust what he had learned from the kind horse whisperer? Or would he need to flee to the fence again and run for a while, until his longing became stronger than his fear? Would repetitive training cement his brand-new trust, or would animal instinct, bred to the bone, require that he question the whisperer's good intent over and over again?

My childhood love for horses had only one rival, and he came to me when I was eight. But he had whispered to me for as long as I could remember. I caught glimpses of him in the wind and the water, in the faces of loved ones, in stars and stillness and games and song. I spoke his name in my "God-blesses," a simple litany of prayers my sister and I recited with our parents each night before we went to sleep. *"God bless Memaw and Pepaw, and Grand Nona and Daddy Mac,"* we'd begin, and then together we'd speak the name of each member of our extended family and ask God to bless them, every one. Later my heart would shape its own free-form prayers, some spoken, some not, but the "God-blesses" were the rote lessons of my devotion, and with them I learned prayer's alphabet so that I could one day speak its language.

God was never a stranger. Church was never a foreign place. The gospel was probably the story that I heard repeated most often in my childhood, so a cynic might argue that I was "marked"—low-hanging fruit for a young and strictly by-the-numbers conversion. But it wasn't like that. It wasn't like anything I'd ever experienced before. It was a magic that blew the doors off Disney without a single special effect.

The One who'd whispered all my life in nature and beauty and Sunday school lessons and repetitive prayer simply began, in the summer of my eighth year, to whisper *my name*. And his voice, after it frightened me by its direct line to my heart and its surprising knowledge of my identity, drew me with what an old prophet called "cords of love." Cords are designed to capture

37

and to keep—but his were not chafing ties or cruel ones. They were cords of pure, irresistible, shining love, and I ached to be held fast by them.

When a Vacation Bible School teacher shared with me the simple facts of the gospel that summer—*For God so loved the world that he gave his only begotten Son, that whosoever believes in him might have everlasting life*—"the world" narrowed to one small girl, and she believed. The information itself was not new. I don't remember anything particularly compelling about this latest reiteration of the truth I had undoubtedly heard before. What *was* new was its power—and its piercing, almost painful impact on a young and mostly unscarred heart. The message ran me straight through before my defenses had had enough time to build up adult-strength resistance.

Every hymn echoed my heart's melody. Every lesson's focus applied to me. And I felt a yearning to respond, to follow, to surrender, that I've never felt so strongly since. If I could have somehow pressed my face into the shoulder of God that July and fallen in behind him like a gentled version of Willy, I would have. I found the voice that I would follow for life, and he spoke my language. Later I would learn bits and pieces of his—but he was bilingual from the start.

My church upbringing—evangelical Protestant, generically speaking, and Southern Baptist to be specific—no doubt eased my introduction to Jesus Christ as Son of God and Savior. But it was outside of the church proper that I learned to hear and recognize his steady, shepherding voice.

Religious practice hardly scratched the surface of the mysterious dynamic Jesus described in John 10 when he said that he calls his own sheep by name and leads them out of the fold, and when he has brought all his own flock outside, he goes in front of them himself, and the sheep follow him because they know his voice. They will never follow a stranger—indeed; they will run away from him, for they do not recognize strange voices. His sheep recognize his voice, and he knows who they are. They follow him and he gives them eternal life. That hearing, I suppose, is tangible enough. The knowing is not.

I've never taken this odd mystery of audible grace for granted, because I've never fully understood it—I've recognized it, like the sheep recognizes his master's voice, but I cannot begin to grasp the meaning of his words. I know better than this very moment's breath that I am his—but I can't reason why that should be so. Actually, it's easier to list the reasons why it should *not* be so. I am stubborn. Weak. Lazy. Latently, inwardly rebellious. Too well trained to be overtly noncompliant, and too cowardly to take Luther's advice and sin "large." I can be impossibly petty, annoyingly demanding, and ruthlessly blunt when tact would better serve. I forget what I should remember and remember what I should forget. I like the last word too much. And that's just for starters.

I know his voice . . . but he knows *me*. He knows the downside I've just described, and the even darker bits I'd never divulge, in person or in print. He inscribes my name on the palm of his hand, saves my tears in a bottle, and rightly numbers the hairs on my head. He remembers me not as a nearly bald, toothless baby in black-and-white photos but as *unformed substance*—as me before the thought of me was known to anyone. And knowing all this, he still chose to call my name.

I have no explanation. None exists. Like the parent who answers her child's "Why?" with a simplistic "Because," God answered my "Why me?" with his profoundly simple "Because I." And that has to be enough. Because after the books are closed and the sermons are done and the theologians have stopped arguing their positions, only two of us will stand face-to-face—he and I.

While I'm confessing, I might as well offer this: The name I heard him call—the one that compelled me to join up with him and follow—was not the name my parents gave to me. It was the name I still don't know. It was the name he gave me, the name that holds in it all the hope of future grace and fits my purchased righteousness like a custom-made glove. It was a name I cannot spell and would dare not even whisper if I knew it, the strange and secret one already written in his great book. And although I did not—do not—know its letters, I knew and heard his voice and believed the name was mine and I was his.

Sometimes the witness of a small wonder can help us to better see a larger one. *Election* and *salvation* and *propitiation* are scholarly words I still struggle to comprehend—but watching the horse whisperer was a felt-board-come-to-life illustration of the call I can't forget. And it reminded me that I am now what my heart has always longed to be: a follower, however hesitant, whose name is known, whose past is precious, and whose future is safe in a gentle pair of hands.

So much of any journey is simply knowing where you started from. The "you are here" red "X" on my spiritual map sits squarely on the South Texas coastline where I lived as a child in the late 1960s. Petula Clark sang "Downtown" on the transistor radio in our kitchen window, and we had a black dachshund named Fritz. My first bike was green, and my best friend's name was Jackie. Conjuring these details helps me to remember where the road began and solidifies the experience in memory.

Where were you when he called your name? How much can you remember about the sights and smells and sounds and textures of that place? When you need to be fortified, to be reassured, to be reminded that you belong . . . go back there. Watch. Listen. As you do, may you hear him whisper your name again, and again, and again.

"He who has an ear, let him hear what the Spirit says to the churches. To him who overcomes, to him I will give some of the hidden manna, and I will give him a white stone, and a new name written on the stone which no one knows but he who receives it" (Rev. 2:17).

"For those whom He foreknew, He also predestined to become conformed to the image of His Son, that He might be the firstborn among many brethren; and these whom He predestined, He also called; and these whom He called, He also justified; and these whom He justified, He also glorified. What then shall we say to these things? If God is for us, who is against us?" (Rom. 8:29–31).

"My sheep hear My voice, and I know them, and they follow Me; and I give eternal life to them, and they will never perish; and no one will snatch them out of My hand" (John 10:27–28).

Beautiful Joe

The Ache of Persevering

If there were any place better for you than the one in which you find yourself, Divine Love would have placed you there.

Charles Spurgeon

Life can be so hard that the temptation to quit or coast tempts us sorely. But there's no joy to be had in stopping short. None. So when God rocks our world, we keep on believing. Not that we'll have our way or that we won't ever experience such awful hurt again. We keep on believing that God knows what he's about. And that, if there *were* any place better for us than the one in which we find ourselves, Divine Love *would* have placed us there.

The first stories I remember began with the words "Once upon a time" and ended neatly with "and they lived happily ever after." For a good while, variations of that theme provided me more than enough reading pleasure. On the lowest shelf of the bookcase in my parents' bedroom was a complete collection of Childcraft volumes with scarlet covers and creamy, gold-embossed bindings, and the stories they contained were read so often by my sister and me that we could easily recite them by heart. But when I was seven and had saved up enough of my allowance to buy the first book of my own choosing, my reading—and my world—became riskier.

That year I discovered *Beautiful Joe*. I took my time selecting it from a long shelf of Whitman children's classics at a Corpus Christi, Texas, variety store, and my memory's a little fuzzy on this, but I think I might have chosen it for its cover. On it a brown mongrel dog with short scraggly hair and badly cropped ears sat on a vine-covered rock. A royal purple banner inscribed with jaunty yellow type hung just above his head. Joe's eyes looked slightly sad, but his mouth was open and his bright pink tongue lolled out in what seemed like a genuine canine smile.

His winsome look made me want to take *Beautiful Joe* home, and I had just enough loose change in my pocketbook to manage it. My parents looked over my selection and nodded their approval, and the purchase was made. I had my new book open in the back seat of the car and had begun to read even before their doors were shut. With the very first words, I was hooked: *"My name is Beautiful Joe, and I am a brown dog of medium size. I am not beautiful, and I am not a thoroughbred. I am only a cur."*

I immediately understood that this Joe, the title character, would be speaking to me directly, telling his story as if he were human. It was his voice I would grow accustomed to, and his "first person" narrative was fiercely compelling to a seven-year-old animal lover. Because his name and his described appearance contradicted one another, I wanted to know who thought Joe was beautiful and why. His first few words had a humility about them that drew me in, for I sensed in my young heart that Beautiful Joe did not *feel* beautiful at all.

Over the next few days, I followed my new friend Joe through trials so terrible I thought my heart would break. I hid my tears as I read, afraid my mother might see me cry and think the book not fit for me—or me for it.

I learned that Joe had been born in the stable of a cruel milkman named Jenkins, who beat and mistreated all the pups in the litter. One rainy day Jenkins drowned all of them but Joe, and soon Joe's own mother died too, leaving him an orphan. He ran away from this mean-tempered man and began a journey that would take him quite far from home and from the only human who had loved him, kind Miss Laura.

He was beaten, lost, and often hungry. More than once I was afraid he might never get home, but I didn't cheat. It never occurred to me to look ahead. I read page after page, hoping, longing, and aching for Joe to find his way back home.

Even when it made me weep, I couldn't put the book away. I had to keep reading because I had begun with Joe and I couldn't bear to leave him midstory. I was afraid to trust completely that the author had "written" him safely home but far too caught up in the tale to close the book and quit. It came to this: I wanted the hoped-for satisfaction of a good and true ending *more* than I wanted the safety of stopping short. I was willing to risk disappointment because my heart was hooked. I was in.

Beautiful Joe taught me one supremely important lesson: the value of sticking with the story, of surrendering control to an invisible author and placing the potential for joy or sadness in his unseen hands.

I also learned from *Beautiful Joe* that an animal, if it is hurt or sick or unhappy, wants its kind master most of all. It loves him or her best and will get better more quickly in his care than anywhere else in the world. Lost dogs want to go home, and they'll endure almost anything to get there. Conflict, tragedy, and loss only make their eventual arrival sweeter.

Joe finally did get home, and as I followed him, word for word and tear for tear, I unknowingly set myself up for a deeper kind of joy. Unknowingly because the true value of heartbreak is mostly invisible until the plot is resolved. Deeper because joy is a weighty thing—and its awesome ballast comes as much from adversity as it does from ease. Maybe more.

The year I first read *Beautiful Joe* I was a mostly carefree second-grader. Life hadn't gotten messy yet, but the lesson was golden. It would keep until I needed it. Later, when my own story became more challenging and my own life's plot more complex, I would remember the long-ago temptation to stop reading *Beautiful Joe*. "Quit here," my fearful heart would beg. "Don't go any further, or you'll be hurt."

But I didn't quit. I followed *Beautiful Joe* all the way to the end, even though I didn't have to. The book, or any subsequent book that saddened or frightened me, could be closed and put away. That is the power we have over our books. We can open them and choose to stay with them to the final sentence . . . or not.

But once we crack a new book's cover and pop its stiff spine and breathe its fresh pages, all bets are off. Once we begin, we run the very real risk of being caught—and held fast—all the way to the bitter end. Any word or phrase or image might be just the one to rattle our brain, prick our heart, or make off with our imagination like the wind carries a hat on a blustery day. Once that critical moment comes, our options have narrowed. The moment the story hooks us, it is the writer, not the reader, who has the upper hand.

Since life (like reading) is fraught with risk, I soon learned a new and subtler way to play it safe. Rather than abandoning the story, I could simply quit feeling its weight. I could begin to look at my own true tale as an aloof, third-person narrator and not its chief protagonist. I could convince myself that I didn't care how any one thing came out and so divorce my heart from the pain of a potentially unhappy ending. I could say I trusted the author but protect myself from his awful power by denying the weight of the story he was crafting. I could choose to lie about my own heart, midstory—not to someone else but to me.

Here's something they mostly forget to tell you in fifth-grade Sunday school: God's people don't get it easy. They don't draw a bye in the hardship tournament, or coast through life in Kevlar vests. They dodge real bullets—lots of them—and sometimes they get hit in the crossfire. When their stories are told in God's book, this hard fact is not left out. We may choose to read around it, but God persists in putting it smack in the middle of the page, *daring* us to detour and refusing to deny that life with him can be one wild and rough ride.

I've heard plenty of sermons on Hebrews 11—faith's who's who—and almost all of them ended at either the pause between verses 12 and 13 or (in a longer version) after the first part of verse 35. It works like this: Up through verse 12 of Hebrews 11, we learn of Abel, Enoch, Noah, and Abraham—how their faith pleased God and they followed him, resulting in "descendents as numerous as the stars in the sky and as countless as the sand on the seashore" (v. 12 NIV).

Abraham and Sarah have a son in their old age, and Isaac becomes the unlikely, long-awaited promise from whom those promised descendants would come. So far, so good.

Then the road takes a bit of a wicked turn: "All these people were still living in faith when they died. They did not receive the things promised; they only saw them and welcomed them from a distance. And they admitted that they were strangers and aliens on earth" (v. 13 NIV).

After that brief, dark pause, there's still more glory: Isaac, Jacob, and Joseph are praised, as is Moses, who we're told regarded disgrace for the sake of Christ to be of greater value than the treasures of Egypt. Rahab's faith gets her a nod, and then other greats of God's story are collectively noted: Gideon, Barak, Samson, Jephthah, Samuel, and the prophets, who "through faith conquered kingdoms, administered justice, and gained what was promised; who shut the mouths of lions, quenched the fury of the flames, and escaped the edge of the sword; whose weakness was turned to strength; and who became powerful in battle and routed foreign armies" (vv. 33–34 NIV). These guys rock, no?

Hold on. Verse 35 resumes this victorious theme, telling us women received their dead, raised to life again, period. But then: "Others were tortured and refused to be released, so that they might gain a better resurrection. Some faced jeers and flogging, while still others were chained and put in prison. They were stoned; they were sawed in two; they were put to death by the sword. They went about in sheepskins and goatskins, destitute, persecuted and mistreated—the world was not worthy of them. They wandered in deserts and mountains, and in caves and holes in the ground. They were all commended for their faith, yet none of them received what had been promised" (vv. 35–39 NIV). Leave it to God to make *Beautiful Joe* seem like a happy fairy tale.

What do we make of this God who has not edited out the hard grit from the drama of his grace? Who instead gives it to us uncut, in a no-holds-barred rush of narrative that would make the strongest of us quiver if we actually believed it?

Life hurts.

Love hurts.

Not everything is settled before we die.

Not everyone dies of old age.

Faith is not an inoculation against hardship.

Christ-followers don't get passed over by pain.

So where does this leave us? It leaves us in the back seat, with the book open and tears falling, too tied-in to stop reading. It leaves us caught midstory. And caught, unwilling to close the book, our options narrow. We can say it doesn't matter to us what happens, but that is a lie. We can harden our hearts so that life's darts don't sting, until eventually we don't even flinch when a stray one hits home. Or we can stick with our story: believing not as much in the hoped-for happy outcome as in the ultimate goodness of the Storyteller.

My friends Mark and Rosemary were the parents of two beautiful children. One awful winter, the younger of them died. Hailey had just turned two when the doctors diagnosed her leukemia. Barely three weeks later, she was gone. These are good people. They love God and follow him—love each other and their children. They are smart and caring, kind and committed. They were a strong, happy family of four, and then suddenly only three of them remained.

After spending a long string of days and nights by their baby girl's bedside, they dug in as her condition worsened and steeled themselves for what they feared most. The doctors did all that they could, much of it difficult for Mark and Rosemary because it was painful for Hailey. No parent wants their child to hurt. No parent wants to allow that hurt, and they will do so only in the hope that it will make the one they love better, stronger, and well. In Hailey's case, it didn't.

Three days after Christmas, these friends held their youngest child in their arms, prayed over her, sang to her, and watched her slip from their arms into the arms of her heavenly Father. How they gathered the courage to endure those few moments I will never know. But they didn't stop loving their daughter when they knew she would be lost. They loved her in the end like they had loved her in the beginning and every day in between. They stuck with the story.

Here's another parent-child story that tears at my heart. Abraham and Sarah have a son, Isaac. God promised this son to them long after nature alone could have delivered on that promise, and they loved him fiercely. He was a good son, and a lot rested on his shoulders. From him, God had said, a nation would arise—a people who would be God's chosen ones and bear his name.

One day God stunned Abraham with these unfathomable words: "Take your son, your only son, Isaac, whom you love, and go to the region of Moriah. Sacrifice him there as a burnt offering on one of the mountains I will tell you about" (Gen. 22:2 NIV). Not fair. Not fair. Not fair. Oh, God, not fair! What good could possibly come of such a thing?

Then, early the next morning, Scripture tells us, Abraham gets up and does as God has commanded him. *Early the next morning.* What must that awful night have been like for this desperate father? Could he hear his son breathing in the tent a few feet away? Did every breath cut him like a knife? Did he lie awake all night and gaze at his precious son's face and form, trying to imprint them in his memory in case tomorrow actually came? Or did he pray to God to take his son's life during the night, if it was required, so that he would not have to raise his hand to him when the sun rose? How crushing this story must have seemed to him in those deep, long hours of the night!

In the morning Abraham climbed Moriah and put his son on the pyre, but when he lifted his knife, God stayed his hand. A ram struggled in the brush nearby, and God made a last-minute substitution that was as baffling as his original command.

That's what happened. Here's what didn't: Abraham never said of Isaac, "I don't love him so very much." Not once. There was no denial spoken to deaden the pain of his required sacrifice. There would have been no point. His heart was already caught—held in taut suspension between the Giver and his good gift—and willing to offer the latter to the former if he must. But not to deny the goodness of the gift. Never that. Not ever.

Abraham had received the improbable promise of his God: a son, an heir, long after it was expected. Hope in any other means had been extinguished. If there was to be a son, God would have to bring him. And God did. Then that same promise-keeping, never-early-but-always-right-on-time God *required* what he had finally given. "That's wrong," my heart protests. "It's just not fair!" Hadn't Abraham showed faith enough in following the Storyteller this far? Couldn't he simply coast now? Didn't he deserve to enjoy this long-awaited blessing unchallenged?

Two stories. Two outcomes. One treasured daughter lost. One promised son spared. No explanation given for either—because God's ways are beyond explaining.

As I sat with Rosemary one afternoon in the hospital, she looked at me and asked, "Do you understand this?" Oh, how I wanted to say yes. But I didn't. I couldn't. Yes would have been a lie.

"No," I said, "I don't."

Then I wanted to say more. To fill up the still air between us with words that would make my "no" less harsh, more comforting. That would make sense of something that made no sense at all. But I had no words. I still don't.

What I do have is an enormous respect for life's unsung heroes: men and women who don't understand, and who hurt, and who suffer stunning losses, and yet persevere by sticking with the story. Who don't curse their own fragile hearts *or* their God. Who don't explain the pain away or deny its terrible hurt. Who continue to love with all the stops out, because that's the only way it's worth doing.

Their stories are part of a larger one, a drama of grace that began in a garden and goes on still. A drama where things are what they seem and more than they seem. Where disaster is disaster but is also an odd means for more of the Author's glory to be displayed.

Even knowing this, trouble can—and sometimes does—cause my faith to waver. Lost opportunities, sickness, death, separation, failure, rejection, and loss . . . all of these raise questions I cannot answer. I know they are not the last word, but they threaten to keep me from sticking with the story.

Like children, we want to skip over life's scary parts, or fast-forward past the terror in our own particular tale. But if we could do so, I suspect we would become not richer but poorer. I imagine God saying to us, midstory, "If you can only trust me in this, the ending will be so much finer and more satisfying."

After all, Beautiful Joe got home.

And so will we. At the culmination of our story, Christ will rule and reign. He will wipe away every tear. Every knee will bow to him, and every tongue *will* call him Lord.

In the meantime, I'll try to trust that each twist and turn along the way will result in God's great glory and my own good. I'll believe that the worst tragedy I could imagine is only the briefest pause in the tale of grace that God whispers in the ears of the sleepy children that he loves. And I'll choose to stick with the story. Because in all its parts, it is the wildest, richest, sweetest one I've known.

C. S. Lewis called pain "God's megaphone to rouse a deaf world," but most of us think our hearing is just fine, thanks. We'd rather not experience God "up close" if that kind of proximity involves pain. But the thing is—we don't get to choose. He's not just the God of the "good life," he's the God of all life.

Are you in a painful place? Has the story taken a turn you didn't expect? Is there a crisis in your life's plot so awful that you wish you could just lie down quietly and despair? Don't. What we think is the end usually isn't. And what we decide is enough heartbreak seldom accurately measures the depth of his mercy and grace. There's more to the story—your story—if you'll only keep watching as he writes. Don't put the book away. Press on. He's far from done, and the ending is sure to fully satisfy.

"Consider it all joy, my brethren, when you encounter various trials, knowing that the testing of your faith produces endurance. And let endurance have its perfect result, so that you may be perfect and complete, lacking in nothing" (James 1:2–4).

"Blessed are the poor in spirit, for theirs is the kingdom of heaven. Blessed are those who mourn, for they shall be comforted. . . . Blessed are those who hunger and thirst for righteousness, for they shall be satisfied" (Matt. 5:2–4, 6).

"And not only this, but we also exult in our tribulations, knowing that tribulation brings about perseverance; and perseverance, proven character; and proven character, hope; and hope does not disappoint, because the love of God has been poured out within our hearts through the Holy Spirit who was given to us" (Rom. 5:3–5).

One Golden Dancing Shoe

The Ache to Celebrate

I wanna dance
I wanna snap my fingers all night long and dance
I wanna move around the room just like a woman in a
  trance
I wanna dance
I wanna wrap my arms around your neck and dance
I wanna listen to the music that's been ringing in my ears
'cause one day I'm gonna dance right out of here.

Derek Webb, "Dance"[1]

It seems I spend half my time looking for the party, and the other half trying to get comfortable with its activity once I've found it. Every now and again something happens to ignite spontaneous celebration, but most days my joy stays well hidden from the naked eye. My bad. God doesn't ask me to keep it down or curb my enthusiasm when his glory peeks through. Just the opposite. And even though the party here is never quite as complete as we'd like, that's no reason to shun it. The next day's redundant sunrise is cause enough to celebrate, especially if you've spent more than a few hours lost in darkness.

*I*n a city of any size, the oddest litter lands in the most improbable places. I've seen bicycles abandoned in spots that were in no way destinations, as if their riders had been raptured up in an instant and given wings instead of wheels. I've spied an intact rocking chair in the center lane of a busy thoroughfare (its owner no doubt circling back to retrieve it) and once an unattended box in a grocery store parking lot that said, "Free puppys, take one." But the most evocative left-behind item of all had to be a single gold lamé party shoe lying in the gutter of a street in my old neighborhood. I still can't shake its image or conjure a story probable enough to explain its random resting place. The shoe trumpeted an incomplete celebration, hinted at an awkward, lopsided dance, and all but begged for a reunion with its missing mate. What good, after all, is one golden dancing shoe?

Maybe the orphaned shoe became stuck in my consciousness because I feel like its distant cousin most days: half dressed for celebration and unsure of where the party might be. Ready to dance, but none too gracefully, given my ill-equipped state. Wishing for a ballroom, a matching shoe, and a night filled with the kind of music (and partner) that could sweep even the clumsiest dancer off her feet. Something inside me suspects I was made for enchanted evenings, even if I am rarely dressed for them. But I can't remember a single anticipated celebration that didn't feel just a little incomplete by its inevitable end.

Few things in a girl's adolescence can compare to the ritual of preparing for a prom or formal dance. Every aspect of the drill is delicious, from the delight of being asked, to dress and shoe shopping, to corsage-pinning, picture-taking, and being gently placed in the passenger side of your date's car like a precious, fragile bloom. The afternoon before my senior prom, my older sister, home from college, painted my toenails while I reclined on the sofa with my feet in her lap. I felt like a princess being made ready for some grand unveiling . . . and I loved the looking-forward-to as much as or more than the event itself. Afterward I would discover the reality that accompanies every "peak" experience: corsages fade, nail polish chips, dresses worn the second time never look quite as lovely as they did the first, and prom dates don't always turn into Prince Charming (sometimes they even tread on your carefully manicured toes).

Dances may disappoint or their best moments fade. But that needn't dull our desire to dance again.

The word translated "celebrate" appears in the Bible nearly forty times. In fact, almost as soon as God called a people for himself and led them out of bondage, he introduced them to the idea of observing special days, or feasts, of celebration. To be a devotee of Yahweh was to be a regular celebrant, and a well-practiced one. The feasts observed by the Jews included the Feast of Unleavened Bread (followed by Passover), the Feast of Weeks (also known as Firstfruits and later Pentecost), the Feast of Trumpets (followed by the annual Day of Atonement), and the Feast of Tabernacles (or booths). Specific instructions for preparation of each of these celebrations were given, down to the tiniest detail. These details themselves were symbolic and commemorative. They recalled God's past history with his people and kept them from forgetting all he had done for them.

In addition to the major feasts, the Jews were required to keep the Sabbath day of each week, the Sabbatical year every seventh year, and the Jubilee year every fiftieth year. Regular feasting and sacrifice were deeply ingrained in the life of every God-follower. And these celebrations were not to be entered into casually or their meaning taken lightly. Over and again God told them, "You shall celebrate," and then he told them *how*. Celebration, it seems, was far too important to be left to chance.

Even before God gave instructions for such observances, men set up altars to remember the places where he had met them. Noah built an altar to the Lord when the ark finally breached on dry ground; Abraham built one at Canaan, where God said to him, "To your descendants I will give this land," and another at Hebron, where he settled for a time. Jacob set up a pillar near the place God appeared to him in a dream and later built an altar over the same spot when God instructed him to do so: "Arise, go up to Bethel and live there, and make an altar there to God, who appeared to you when you fled from your brother Esau" (Gen. 35:1).

We observe "structured" celebrations too, when good things happen to us. We commemorate birthdays and anniversaries, wedding days and holidays. These regular red-letter days keep our celebratory "muscles" limber and warm—ready to spring into play when joy calls for not just a shout but a full-on dance. And we have our "ad hoc" celebrations as well: home plate high-fives and end zone boogies, "It's a girl!" banners in front yards, or candlelit cakes delivered by serenading waiters.

Whatever the occasion, the very best celebrations seamlessly connect two realities: the seen with the unseen, the past with the future, a promise with its fulfillment. And by doing so, they transform their participants. Weddings especially have the power to achieve this; not only does a wedding signal the transformation of a betrothed couple into a new husband and wife team, it can invite every married man and woman who witness the newlyweds'

vows to say "yes" to each other all over again, in spite of what they now know about the trials and rigors of one-flesh living.

Even a single meal celebrated among friends possesses the hidden power to change lives, as Isak Dinesen's tale *Babette's Feast* so beautifully demonstrates. In Dinesen's fable, after Babette is widowed in Paris, she travels to a cold, inhospitable village in Denmark to live with two spinster sisters. She carries a letter of introduction that says simply, "Babette knows how to cook," and for fourteen years she dutifully prepares nothing more than the simple steamed fish and ale-and-bread broth that Martine and Philippa are accustomed to. But one day Babette receives a letter saying she has won ten thousand francs in the French lottery, and she asks the sisters if she may prepare for them a "proper French dinner." They agree and invite a handful of neighbors, most of them feuding with each other, who arrive determined not to make much of the rich food placed before them or to let Babette's festive table take the edge off their bitterness against one another.

But theirs is a losing battle.

Babette lays a table with exquisite china and stemware and serves fine French wine and course after course of lovely, mouth-watering food. A huge tortoise gives its life for the soup course, and a cageful of tiny quail become *caille en sarcophage*, their frail bodies roasted in delicate pastry "coffins" and dressed with rich sauce. *Blinis demidoff*, feather light cake, huge rounds of cheese, and colorful, ripe fruit are offered. The diners' stern faces soften with each amazing dish, and sworn enemies smilingly eye one another over their gleaming plates and glasses. The guest of honor, a visiting army general, gently taps his glass near the close of the meal and rises to declare,

> Mercy and truth have met together; righteousness and bliss shall kiss one another. Man, in his weak shortsightedness, believes he must make choices in his life. He trembles at the risks he takes . . . but our choice is of no importance. There comes a time when your

eyes are opened, and we come to realize that mercy is infinite. We need only await it with confidence and receive it with gratitude. Mercy imposes no conditions. And lo! Everything we have chosen has been granted to us, and everything we have rejected has also been granted, for mercy and truth have met together. Righteousness and bliss shall kiss one another.[2]

Then the gathered celebrants depart, but not before joining hands and singing a hymn together which ends with the words, "Never would You give a stone to the child who asks for bread."[3] Standing in the cold outside the humble home where they feasted on such an extravagant meal, one guest looks to the sky and remarks in a reverent voice, "The stars have moved closer. Perhaps they move closer every night."[4] Babette's lavish and loving feast awakened their numbed senses to a beauty and joy they had almost forgotten.

The sisters go back inside to praise a happy but exhausted Babette and to ask her when she will return to France as a chef (since obviously someone with so much skill could not be expected to remain another day in their backwater Danish village). She replies that she is going nowhere. Every franc she'd won, Babette had gladly and joyfully spent on the lavish meal they'd just consumed. The fact that the next day she would return to serving fish and broth for two aging sisters in no way diminished her joy at having crafted a feast worthy of a king. Her celebration had healed old wounds, reconciled feuding friends, and warmed every heart at the table. Her gift had powerfully transformed a single meal into a love affair, if only for a few precious hours. And she deemed such celebration a worthy and wholly satisfying expense.

The first recorded miracle or sign of the Son of God took place at a wedding celebration. Jesus, his mother, and his disciples were invited to a wedding in Cana of Galilee, and this festive occasion became the backdrop for a never-before-seen wonder. John, present at the scene, records what took place in the Gospel that bears his name: "When the wine gave out, the mother of Jesus said to Him, 'They have no wine.' And Jesus said to her, 'Woman, what does that have to do with us? My hour has not yet come'" (John 2:3–4). Mary was clearly asking Jesus to do something about the problem—and she was convinced that he could. When he demurred, she told the servants responsible for the food, "Whatever He says to you, do it" (v. 5).

An Eastern wedding celebration with no more wine was a catastrophe in the making. When the food and wine ran out, the party was essentially over. And it was not yet time for the feasting to end. The absence of wine would reflect badly on the host and drain the joy from the bridal couple and their guests. Into this dilemma comes one who is able to transform the dying party into an even finer feast. Mary may have known her son's true identity, but to others, his glory was still "under wraps." He had not yet come out publicly as the Son of God. But this act, and this day, would begin to change that.

"Now there were six stone waterpots set there for the Jewish custom of purification, containing twenty or thirty gallons each. Jesus said to [the servants], 'Fill the waterpots with water.' So they filled them up to the brim. And He said to them, 'Draw some out now and take it to the headwaiter'" (John 2:6–8). They did, and at some point between the drawing of the water and its presentation to the headwaiter, its physical properties were transformed. It became wine. And not just any old wine. *Excellent wine.*

"When the headwaiter tasted the water which had become wine, and did not know where it came from (but the servants who had drawn the water knew), the headwaiter called the bridegroom, and said to him, 'Every man serves the good wine first, and when the people have drunk freely, then he serves the poorer wine; but you have kept the good wine until now" (John 2:9–10). Not only did the party continue to roll and the bridegroom avoid embarrassment, but life was injected into the festivities by the appearance of such good and excellent provision. And not only did Jesus transform a common liquid into a fine, fermented wine, he also showed the first public glimmer of his glory and transformed those closest to him—his disciples—into *believing* followers, not simply curious ones. There, in the dusty town of Cana, mercy and truth met together, and heaven and earth drew closer to one another.

The Savior's presence transformed that ancient celebration, taking it to another level altogether. His presence today does likewise. "In Your presence," the psalmist writes, "is fullness of joy; in Your right hand there are pleasures forever" (Ps. 16:11). Jesus came, he insisted, so that we might have life—and not mediocre life or fearful life but *abundant* life. *Life worth celebrating.*

I confess to being a cautious celebrator. I don't want to be. But I'm afraid if I throw myself completely into joy, I may be embarrassed. If I acknowledge that something is wonderful—if I do the happy dance in front of others—the thing that inspired my celebration may disappear before my eyes and leave me feeling very, very foolish. My slightly melancholy personality may have equipped me better for contemplation, or even lament, and causes me to check my exuberance before things get too out of hand—even when I'd prefer not to.

But God doesn't ask me to do that. In fact, he invites my celebration and my joy when he is the source of it. His presence in my life makes celebration a perfectly reasonable and right response. The feasts and celebrations of God's people before the coming of Christ were merely the foreshadowing of his glorious arrival and his atoning sacrifice. Because of him, righteousness and bliss really do kiss one another in full view of everyone—and joy transforms every celebration where he is the guest of honor.

My young friend Amanda married her husband John in a beautiful candlelight ceremony. I've known Amanda since she was a little red-headed girl, and she has grown into a lovely, energetic, godly woman. Her wedding was an elegant and extremely formal affair. And Amanda was the wiggliest bride I have ever seen in my life. As she stood before the minister facing her husband-to-be, Amanda literally shimmied and hopped from one foot to another in pure, unchecked delight. She held John's hands and gazed into his face as they spoke their vows, but she simply could not keep still from the neck down. She had waited for this moment all her life, and she could not contain her joy.

Even though the wedding was formal and hundreds of people were watching, no one minded Amanda's impromptu wedding-day dance—especially not John! (What groom in his right mind would be bothered by a woman so excited to marry him that she couldn't keep herself still?) Her celebration didn't take away from the occasion—it added to it! Her pleasure in the presence of her groom lit not only his face but every face in the room.

The vows these two spoke to one another were not giddy; they were solemn. They promised to love and cherish each other in the good and not-so-good days ahead, rich or poor, sick or well, for better or worse. Their marriage would not be perfect (no marriage is). But the impossibility of a perfect marriage in no way diminished Amanda's wedding-day joy. Not one bit. Knowing that anything could go wrong, that tomorrow could dawn dark and cold, and that all sorts of ills could befall the two of them in an evil and fallen world—little Amanda danced anyway!

You and I have the groom above all grooms. Our beloved has wooed us and won us. We are his, and he is ours. He has paid our bride price, claimed us as his own, and gone to prepare a place for us. Can you imagine a better reason to celebrate? He has not yet returned for us, that is true. And we are not immune from sorrow or heartache or sickness or poverty as we wait for him. But nothing, nothing at all, can separate us from his love: "But in all these things we overwhelmingly conquer through Him who loved us. For I am convinced that neither death, nor life, nor angels, nor principalities, nor things present, nor things to come, nor powers, nor height, nor depth, nor any other created thing, will be able to separate us from the love of God, which is in Christ Jesus our Lord" (Rom. 8:37–39).

We may not be fully equipped for the party to come, or even for the lesser activities leading up to the big event, but that should not keep us from dancing with him when the occasion calls for celebration. Our groom has come. He will come again. One shoe or two, two left feet or the grace of a ballerina, a beautiful gown or an old pair of jeans, he extends his hand and invites us into his presence, where there is fullness of joy. "Dance with me," he invites. And only a fool would decline.

A precious friend of mine died at the age of ninety-one, more fully in love with Jesus than she had been at nine or thirty-nine or eighty-nine. As she grew weaker and weaker, ministers with whom she had once served would visit her in the hospital to encourage her to get well. "We need you at the church," one of them said to her in an effort to lift her spirits. He needn't have wasted his breath. "Don't

you pray me back," she said. "I've got someplace to go." When he told me this, I asked him, "How did she look?" And this is what he said to me: "Like a girl getting ready for her first date." She had not turned down a single one of her Lover's invitations to dance. And she wasn't about to begin, so close to the party for which she'd waited a lifetime.

Celebrating is only risky if the source of our joy is uncertain. Friends will let us down (and we'll disappoint them too). Vacations will fail to measure up to the promise of their postcards. Jobs will become dull and routine, and even the best marriages will at times seem like a whole lot of work and not much reward. But our Savior-King is a strong and certain joy whose presence will never disappoint. And he doesn't mind our clumsiness one bit as he leads us out onto the floor. So what do you say? The King is asking. Will you dance?

"While they were eating, Jesus took some bread, and after a blessing, He broke it and gave it to the disciples, and said, 'Take, eat; this is My body.' And when He had taken a cup and given thanks, He gave it to them, saying 'Drink from it, all of you; for this is My blood of the covenant, which is poured out for many for forgiveness of sins. But I say to you, I will not drink of this fruit of the vine from now on until that day when I drink it new with you in My Father's kingdom'" (Matt. 26:26–29).

"My flesh and my heart may fail, but God is the strength of my heart and my portion forever. For, behold, those who are far from You will perish; You have destroyed all those who are unfaithful to You. But as for me, the nearness of God is my good; I have made the Lord God my refuge, that I may tell of all Your works" (Ps. 73:26–28).

"For Christ our Passover also has been sacrificed. Let us therefore celebrate the feast, not with old leaven, nor with the leaven of malice and wickedness, but with the unleavened bread of sincerity and truth" (1 Cor. 5:7–8).

The Front Porch Castaway

The Ache for Adventure

Men wanted for hazardous journey. Small wages, bitter cold, long months of complete darkness, constant danger, safe return doubtful. Honor and recognition in case of success.

Sir Ernest Shackleton

The games we played as children were almost always about adventure. We named our favorite superheroes early and imitated them with devoted abandon. Forts were built, heroines rescued, and dragons slain as if courage were a cornflakes additive, never in short supply. When did we learn to ignore the lure of the venturing conquest? When did we begin to prize our safety over a morning sail out into the bright unknown?

A torrential overnight rain brought a surprising morning visitor to my door. Between the hedge and the bottom step of the front porch a yellow rubber duck lay marooned, far from home, and from the looks of it, his journey had been a wild one. The storms of the previous evening had scattered leaves and small branches across the yard. What shrubs were still blooming now stood beaten down and bent, their drenched flowers sadly torn. The duck himself was upended and muddy, with one wet leaf plastered across his back like a slippery saddle.

No small children lived nearby, so this particular ducky must have come a long way—carried by the wind, or the water, or both. He was far from the bathtub or baby pool he'd almost certainly been bought to sail—and he looked decidedly worse for the ride. I picked him up with the intention of discarding him with the rest of the storm's debris . . . but I couldn't. He'd seen so much trouble that the trash seemed insulting, so I rinsed him off instead and tucked him back beneath the step. Courage in the face of danger, I decided, was a thing to be rewarded—not lightly tossed away.

The front porch castaway didn't choose his storm. The storm chose him. The safer existence was no doubt the one he'd left behind. But he'd survived the night's odd exodus, and his story, even untold, *had* to be a richer one for that wild ride.

I grew up wanting to *go.* Family lore has it that my favorite rocking horse was ridden to death, its springs finally sprung from one too many living room gallops. When I wasn't on my horse, I sat on the floor or in a chair and rocked myself back and forth: constant motion in a pair of footie-pajamas. When I could be outside I was. No tree was too tall to climb; no stray cat was too unfriendly to pet; no puddle, pool, or creek was too cold to test with at least one toe. If someone was going, I wanted to go too. Mine was the "shotgun" seat in the family car, whether the trip was to the grocery store or the garbage dump. If there was motion anywhere, I made sure I was in its wake.

Adventure—any adventure—was infinitely more preferable to me than the predictable routine. The unknown held more allure than the ordinary. It still does. I'm mystified by those who don't care to see those things they haven't yet seen, visit the places they haven't yet been, or taste the events they've only heard of but not yet experienced. I can't imagine loving management more than mystery or choosing more of the same over surprise—and I don't think I'm entirely alone. Each of us carries a little of the explorer within. Whether it's well developed or well hidden, we harbor a small, insistent voice that asks, "Isn't there something *more*?"

The ad in London newspapers in early 1900 read, "Men wanted for hazardous journey. Small wages, bitter cold, long months of complete darkness, constant danger, safe return doubtful. Honor and recognition in case of success." It was placed by British explorer Sir Ernest Shackleton in preparation for his National Arctic Expedition, which subsequently failed to reach the South Pole. But despite its foreboding tone, the advertisement received an astronomical number of replies, prompting Shackleton to note: "It seemed as though all the men in Great Britain were determined to accompany me, the response was so overwhelming."[1]

Shackleton sought men to join him on a hazardous journey. But he wasn't the first to make such a call. Centuries before, Jesus said to those men showing interest in his mission: "If anyone wishes to come after Me, let him deny himself, and take up his cross and follow Me. For whoever wishes to save his life will lose it; but whoever loses his life for My sake will find it. For what will it profit a man if he gains the world and forfeits his soul?" (Matt. 16:24–26).

The call of Christ is nothing less than a call to adventure. Jesus gave no quiet invitation to a life of ease or sofa-sitting or safe observation. He issued a daring challenge to live a life with no boundaries and no guarantees. Well . . . perhaps one guarantee: There *will* be trouble. "When Christ calls a man," said German martyr Dietrich Bonhoeffer, "he bids him come and die."

Even as we long for adventure, the pragmatist in each of us reasons that to go after more of life may only invite more pain or suffering. And our inner pragmatist is right. It will. Christ-followers may opt for the observer's role to avoid danger, but Jesus was clear: seek to save your life and you're sure to lose it. Play "fast and loose" with it for his sake, and it will be forever found. Shortly before he was betrayed, arrested, tried, and executed, the Son of God let his followers know that they were in for perilous times if they stayed the course: "If the world hates you, you know that it has hated Me before it hated you. If you were of the world, the world would love its own; but because you are not of the world, but I chose you out of the world, because of this the world hates you. Remember the word that I said to you, 'A slave is not greater than his master.' If they persecuted Me, they will also persecute you; if they kept My word, they will keep yours also. But all these things they will do to you for My name's sake, because they do not know the One who sent Me" (John 15:18–21).

Could he have been any more blunt? "If the world persecuted me," he said, "it will persecute you." Period. Following Christ doesn't afford us an "invisibility cloak" (à la *Harry Potter* and

The Lord of the Rings) against suffering. It's more like erecting a lightning rod for it.

Those who did continue following hard after him learned that Jesus had told them the truth. They did not live quiet lives and die quiet deaths. They got off the porch. They braved the night storms. They answered the call to adventure. And they would never be the same.

Even as we try to stuff it down, our passion for adventure and daring rises up to betray us. We flock to movies that reek of it: *Saving Private Ryan. Gladiator. Braveheart. The Lord of the Rings. Master and Commander.* The main characters in each of these stories loved and valued something more than their own safety and relative ease.

The first time I saw the modern film version of Shakespeare's *Henry V*, I was moved by its call to bold living. I'm a woman, not a warrior; a storyteller, not a soldier—and yet the words of young King Harry on the eve of his greatest battle stirred something in me I'd felt before but could not name. Outnumbered by the French forces at Agincourt, Henry's men are sick, tired, and frightened. The French call for his surrender, but Henry refuses: "We would not seek a battle, as we are; nor as we are, we say, we will not shun it."[2]

His loyal subject Westmoreland notes their depleted ranks and says wistfully, "O that we had here just one ten thousand of those men in England who do no work today." But Harry will have none of that, arguing, "No, my fair cousin: If we are mark'd to die, we are enough to do our country loss; and if to live, the fewer men, the greater share of honour. God's will! I pray thee, wish not one man more."[3]

Then he begins the now-famous speech that had me ready to enlist before he paused for breath even the first time:

This day is called the feast of Crispian:
He that outlives this day, and comes safe home,
Will stand a tip-toe when the day is named,
And rouse him at the name of Crispian.
He that shall live this day, and see old age,
Will yearly on the vigil feast his neighbours,
And say 'Tomorrow is Saint Crispian:'
Then will he strip his sleeve and show his scars
And say 'These wounds I had on Crispian's day.'
Old men forget: yet all shall be forgot,
But he'll remember with advantages
What feats he did that day; then shall all our names
Familiar in his mouth as household words—
Harry the king, Bedford and Exeter,
Warwick and Talbot, Salisbury and Gloucester,
Be in their flowing cups freshly remember'd.
This story shall the good man teach his son;
And Crispin Crispian shall ne'er go by,
From this day to the ending of the world,
But we in it shall be remember'd.
We few, we happy few, we band of brothers;
For he to-day that sheds his blood with me
Shall be my brother, be he ne'er so vile,
This day shall gentle his condition.
And gentlemen in England now a-bed
Shall think themselves accursed they were not here,
And hold their manhoods cheap whilst any speaks
That fought with us upon Saint Crispin's day.[4]

I knew I was hearing something extraordinary . . . and something I'd heard before, however faint: the call to live beyond myself. The call to spend myself for something greater than my own pleasure or gain. The call to the daring adventure of high-stakes living, with all its attendant risks and glories. My heart had long been asking, "Isn't there more than this?" and the drama on the screen before me was reminding me that the answer was a resounding "Yes!"

What calls us to more—more adventure, more risk, more striving—is the simple belief that *more exists*. What beckons us beyond comfort is the promise of a King who gives us glimpses of his blazing kingdom wrapped in the tissue-thin cover of present reality. He calls whom he calls, when he wills. And when he does call, the invitation is all but irresistible.

The man Abram and his wife Sarai were probably content in Haran. Then one day God came calling. "Now the LORD said to Abram, 'Go forth from your country, and from your relatives and from your father's house, to the land which I will show you; and I will make you a great nation, and I will bless you, and make your name great; and so you shall be a blessing; and I will bless those who bless you, and the one who curses you I will curse. And in you all the families of the earth shall be blessed'" (Gen. 12:1–3).

Abram's father Terah had died. His wife Sarai was barren. His nuclear family had not long before relocated from a place called Ur. Abram was not in a venturing out frame of mind. He was settled . . . or so he must have thought. Then God called him out of Haran and into a place known only as "the land which I will show you." (I might have immediately requested map coordinates; Abram, to his credit, did not.) At an age when he might have been justified in taking his ease, Abram was invited by God out of self-sufficiency and into dependence. He was urged beyond fact and into faith. And in faith he went: "So Abram went forth as the LORD had spoken to him; and Lot went with him. Now Abram was seventy-five years old when he departed from Haran. And Abram took Sarai his wife and Lot his nephew, and all their possessions which they had accumulated, and the persons which they had acquired in Haran, and they set out for the land of Canaan; thus they came to the land" (Gen. 12:4–5).

Interesting thing about "the land" God called Abram to: It was already inhabited! Abram's great adventure was not a graceful waltz into an open pasture but a steady march into enemy territory. Once again, God called him aside and spoke: "To your descendants I will give this land" (Gen. 12:7). The fact that Abram *had* no descendents at the time was of little consequence. God was promising as if Abram were already the father of a brood. Famine drove Abram from Canaan to Egypt and from Egypt to the Negev. He separated from his brother-in-law Lot and finally settled in the land of Canaan while Lot "moved his tents as far as Sodom" (Gen. 13:12). Thus fixed, Abram heard from God again: "Now lift up your eyes and look from the place where you are, northward and southward and eastward and westward; for all the land which you see, I will give it to you and to your descendants forever" (Gen. 13:14–15).

Because he and Sarai still had no children, Abram suggested that perhaps another male in his household could be "counted" as his offspring, so as to fulfill God's promises, but God reaffirmed his prior word to Abram with a little nighttime show-and-tell: "And He took him outside and said, 'Now look toward the heavens, and count the stars, if you are able to count them.' And He said to him, 'So shall your descendants be.' Then he believed in the LORD; and He reckoned it to him as righteousness" (Gen. 15:5–6).

Perhaps you know the rest of the story. Abram and Sarai become impatient and try to expedite the plan of God by using their maid Hagar as a "rented womb." Hagar becomes pregnant by Abram and has a son named Ishmael. But surrogate parenting wasn't God's plan, and Ishmael wasn't God's man. So when Abram is ninety-nine years old, God comes calling again: "I am

God Almighty; walk before Me, and be blameless. I will establish My covenant between Me and you, and I will multiply you exceedingly" (Gen. 17:1–2).

Arguably, Abram should have learned by this time that when Infinity pours out blessing, there's always an overflow; that when God makes promises, he means to keep them. But would you have been any easier than Abram to convince? I might have wavered too—or tried the do-it-yourself-heir program long before he and Sarai resorted to it. God insisted, however, that his original plan for Abram and Sarai was still in play and by no means transferable: "As for Me, behold, My covenant is with you, and you will be the father of a multitude of nations. No longer shall your name be called Abram, but your name shall be Abraham; for I have made you the father of a multitude of nations. I will make you exceedingly fruitful, and I will make nations of you, and kings will come forth from you. I will establish my covenant between Me and you and your descendants after you throughout their generations for an everlasting covenant, to be God to you and to your descendants after you" (Gen. 17:4–7).

When God called Abram at the beginning, he said only, "Come out to a land which I will show you." And with that little bit of instruction, Abram followed. Later he would get more information and even a new name. His calling would be refined and reiterated over time. He would learn more of what God had in mind at the start. He would discover that the plan wasn't limited to him but included his descendents as well. And he would learn that Almighty God is quite unfazed by obstacles like infertility and aging, famine, occupied land, and opposing armies.

His wife Sarai would receive a new name too and more specifics about that "heir" business God had been speaking of for so long: "As for Sarai your wife, you shall not call her name Sarai, but Sarah shall be her name. I will bless her, . . . and she shall be the mother of nations; kings of peoples shall come from her" (Gen. 17:15–16). Abraham wasn't so sure God was good for his promise if its fulfillment depended on Abraham and his nearly-one-hundred-year-old wife: "Then Abraham fell on his face and laughed, and said in his heart, 'Will a child be born to a man one hundred years old? And will Sarah, who is ninety years old, bear a child?' And Abraham said to God, 'Oh, that Ishmael might live before You!' But God said, 'No, but Sarah your wife will bear you a son, and you shall call his name Isaac; and I will establish My covenant with him for an everlasting covenant for his descendants after him'" (Gen. 17:15–19).

Late in their great adventure, Abraham and Sarah did indeed have a son, Isaac. And all the nations were indeed blessed by their eventual offspring, including Jacob, Judah, Obed, Jesse, David . . . and finally the covenant-keeper whose name was Jesus. There was more, much more, at stake at Abraham's first "yes" than a life of stability and security in the land of Haran. There was more, much more, to be experienced for this childless couple than a comfortable drift into retirement age. Abraham was called into the wild adventure of God's unfolding plan. And he went.

Who knows whether it was the commanding sound of God's voice, or the one-night-only star show, or the first glimpse of Canaan's beauty that kept Abraham "venturing out"? This much we are told: "By faith Abraham, when he was called, obeyed by going out to a place which he was to receive for an inheritance; and he went out, *not knowing where he was going.* By faith he lived as an alien in the land of promise, as in a foreign land, dwelling in tents with Isaac and Jacob, fellow heirs of the same promise" (Heb. 11:8–9, emphasis added).

Abraham's lesson to me is this: no great faith . . . no great adventure. If I don't *believe* God, I am unlikely to follow him far. Adventuring requires that I trust what I cannot see and that I remain confident in the leading and the promises of God, even before I experience their reality. Adventuring demands that I not make myself too much at home in any one place—and that I am willing to move out from that place when he calls. Adventuring asks that I agree with God that this world is not my natural home—a very odd thing when you think of it. After all, I was born here. I'm a "native," so to speak, but I am not operating as such. If I were, I'd have an easier time of things. I'd know the "lingo" better and adapt more freely to my surroundings. My foreigner status wouldn't be given away time and again by my ignorance of certain things or my out-of-sync walk or talk.

Even though this world is *not* my home, and even though I crave adventure, I confess that I also have a fondness for the left-hand side of my couch, where my dog sleeps in my lap and a soft blanket warms my feet. Where I can open a book and "travel" to a mysterious destination without the risks of "complete darkness, constant danger, or [doubtful] safe return." Where I can relax and be comfortably entertained. An unrelenting tension exists between what I desire and what I actually *dare*—even on my boldest days. "All around us," said G. K. Chesterton, "is the city of small sins, abounding in backways and retreats, but surely, sooner or later, the towering flame will rise from the harbour announcing that the reign of the cowards is over and a man is burning his ships."[5]

The only place I truly belong is the place to which God calls me. My salvation has rendered me an alien in this world, a front porch castaway whose journey—if she sets her ships afire—will be shaped by something infinitely braver, wilder, and stronger than herself.

Where do you feel most at home? Sam and Frodo loved the Shire, but they traveled far from it when adventure beckoned. The Pevensie children loved England best—until Narnia (and Aslan!) captured their hearts. Are you willing to concede that the place you call home may not

be home at all, but only the best glimmer of it you've seen yet? If God calls you past the place where you've comfortably settled, will you trust him enough to "go out, not knowing," in obedience and in faith?

The apostle Paul said that his great aim in life was to know Christ—in the power of his resurrection and the fellowship of his suffering. To do that, he willingly traveled with Christ, wherever Christ bid him go. Adventure, to Paul, meant the constant presence of Christ, and in any locale, in any situation, he longed to be conformed to the image of his beautiful Savior. Could you learn to savor that kind of adventure?

"By faith Abraham, when he was called, obeyed by going out to a place which he was to receive for an inheritance; and he went out, not knowing where he was going. By faith he lived as an alien in the land of promise, as in a foreign land, dwelling in tents with Isaac and Jacob, fellow heirs of the same promise; for he was looking for the city which has foundations, whose architect and builder is God" (Heb. 11:8–10).

"If anyone wishes to come after Me, he must deny himself, and take up his cross and follow Me. For whoever wishes to save his life will lose it; but whoever loses his life for My sake will find it" (Matt. 16:24–25).

"As He was going along by the Sea of Galilee, He saw Simon and Andrew, the brother of Simon, casting a net in the sea; for they were fishermen. And Jesus said to them, 'Follow Me, and I will make you become fishers of men.' Immediately they left their nets and followed Him" (Mark 1:16–18).

"Have Courage"

The Ache to Hear God

Maybe the still small voice we are waiting to hear is already whispering in the details of our lives—especially the details we wish would go away and leave us alone.

Thomas Schmidt, *A Scandalous Beauty*[1]

Who doesn't hope to hear a word from heaven? Who doesn't wish that a knowing voice would whisper truth or comfort or direction or encouragement when it is needed most? We long to hear from God. We want to know he's with us. We pine for a sign or a sound or some well-placed punctuation that says he's nearer than we can tell. That he sees. He knows. But how do you learn to listen for the wind?

We called the game "gossip." One child in a circle of children would whisper a sentence to the one closest to him or her. Then that one would whisper what they'd just heard to the next one, then the next. No repeating for clarity's sake. No "do-overs." We listened once as intently as we could, then repeated carefully what we believed we'd heard. When the words had passed to and through each child, the last one (sitting just inches from the first) would speak the sentence out loud. And every time, the one who'd started the game going would correct its inevitable mangling with, "Oh no! What I *said* was . . ."

No matter how hard we tried, no matter how attentive we'd been, the message was always altered a lot or a little in the passing along. The whispering probably didn't help. Perceptions certainly shaded our various interpretations. None of us was 100 percent sure about what we'd heard, but we did the best we could to make sense of it and pass it along correctly. If the process had worked flawlessly, there would have been no game. It didn't—and back then at least, that was the fun of "gossip."

Back then our circle was small, and we spoke the same language. We lived on the same block and played on the same playground. We knew each other's names and favorite colors and siblings and funniest stories. We were comfortably familiar with one another, and still we garbled the details, even if we got the gist.

So is it any wonder we struggle to hear aright—or hear at all—the God of the universe when he speaks?

If he were only the God who *has* spoken, we could depend on history's record alone. We could rely exclusively on what *others* say he said and cease to listen for ourselves. If he were done communicating, we could be done listening. But he's not—so we can't be either. If ours were a God who always spoke in the same way, through the same means, we might be helped a little more. But his range is immeasurable, and his methods are a moving target: He is, after all, the one who convened a fireside chat with Moses via a burning desert bush, who directed Balaam's attention by the very donkey he was riding on, who knocked Saul off his horse with the sound of his voice, and who called to young Samuel in his sleep.

When he did speak directly, the effect was so terrifying, so stunning, so showstopping that he began almost every utterance with the words "Fear not." Because, of course, to hear—actually hear—the one who spoke the worlds into being in a voice not unlike your neighbor's would *more* than give one heart-hammering pause. Where speech is concerned, God is indeed the biggest bull in earth's china shop, the towering giant in this land of ants, whose voice is as likely to wreak havoc as it is to command respect. Such greatness must come at us indirectly, or else enter saying "Fear not," so as not to frighten us half to death. We want to hear from him, yes—but the possibility that he might address us one-to-one is enough to undo even the bravest of us.

Yet from the beginning he has spoken. And he is speaking still. "God," said the writer of Hebrews, "after He spoke long ago to the fathers in the prophets in many portions and in many ways, in these last days has spoken to us in His Son" (Heb. 1:1–2). The Bible records for us the words of the Father and the Son and promises still more speech from the third person of the Trinity, the Holy Spirit: "But when He, the Spirit of truth, comes, He will guide you into all the truth; for He will not speak on His own initiative, but whatever He hears, He will speak; and He will disclose to you what is to come. He will glorify Me; for He will take of Mine and will disclose it to you" (John 16:13–15).

The Bible assures me that the God I love is a speaking God. And because he is, I should expect to hear from him in whatever way he sees fit to address me. So far he has been quite tender in his speech. I suspect he knows I'm not up for anything quite as direct as "Greetings, favored one! The Lord is with you" (Luke 1:28) or "I who speak to you am He" (John 4:26). He restrains from overwhelming me with more of himself than I can stand, until I can stand it. Emily Dickinson described it thus: "He fumbles at your Soul/As Players at the Keys/Before they drop full Music on/He stuns you by degrees."[2]

I long for his voice; I fear it too. I want to know he's near, but the reality of his presence when I am aware of it is almost too much to bear. So he mercifully stuns me degree by degree with his well-placed words of life—whether they are spoken or not.

My first trip to England was drawing to a close, and I was thrilled to have traveled on my own and to have followed this ambitious agenda while I was there: Do more of whatever it is you're afraid of. I had walked into a pub alone and ordered up ridiculous-sounding bangers and mash for dinner; punted a flat-bottomed boat on the River Cherwell; survived a midnight solo ride with a London cabbie; and read a freshly created monologue to a roomful of people I'd never met. I'd eaten unidentifiable things for breakfast and approached total strangers for directions. (After a few days, I'd even *given* strangers directions!)

When the adventure-filled week and a half came to a close, though, I was equally thrilled to be going home. I had planned to take a bus from Oxford into London, then make a quick "tube" trip from Paddington Station to Gatwick to board my nonstop flight to Houston. I had checked the bus schedules the day before, and I arrived at the bus stop on a Saturday morning with little time to spare. But as the minutes ticked by, the bus did not arrive. When I examined the posted schedule again, I realized I'd written down the *weekday* departure times, not those for the weekend. And I had wasted nearly half an hour waiting for a bus that wasn't coming!

Because my beautifully constructed "plan A" was now rendered inoperable, I did what I had not done once in the ten days previous: I panicked. What if I couldn't get to the station in time? What if I missed my flight? What if I had to stay over another night or more, or pay some exorbitant rate for rebooking my return? With my heart in my throat I began walking from the bus station to the Oxford train depot, where I quickly bought a ticket for the next train heading to London. I say "heading" there, because it never gained much momentum, stopping at every station in between. Somewhere around the third or fourth stop, I was nearing a meltdown. I had not been anxious even once since I'd left home, and now cold fear was swallowing me up. I lowered my eyes to the floor and did what I should have begun doing several miles earlier: I prayed.

When I opened my eyes, the train was slowing slightly. I glanced out the window. We were approaching the town of Reading, and there on the side of an old brick building were painted these words: *Have Courage.* I had just prayed for help, and as near as I could tell, God's answer to my fearful pleading was simply this: *Have Courage.* "London: around the next bend" might have been more informative and reassuring, but that wasn't what I got. I got *Have Courage.*

So I took courage. I thanked him for what I thought might have been a supernatural sign. But my bolstered courage didn't last long. I kept looking at my watch and thinking, *I'm not going to make it in time. I'm really not going to make it.* Sweat trickled down my ribs, and I had a sick feeling in my stomach. I was doing what I was afraid of, all right. But definitely *not* by design. I began again to pray, only this time I didn't lower my head or close my eyes. We slowed as we approached the next small town, and once more, incredibly, I saw painted on the side of another building the same message as before: *Courage.*

I didn't know whether to laugh or cry. "Okay, God," I prayed. "I hear you. I needed a word from you, and you gave one. I get it. I *do* take courage in you. You know what needs to happen here, so even if I miss my flight and have to spend the night on a train station bench, I trust you. I'm not afraid. I have courage—no, I'm *taking* courage—in you."

Just over an hour later, I arrived at Gatwick with time to spare. Not much time but enough. And I made it home on the flight I might have missed, convinced that if I had taken the train *back* to Oxford, past the towns I'd traveled through, my "courage" messages would have mysteriously disappeared.

A year or so later, I was reading a book called *Beginning* by Irish actor Kenneth Branagh. In it he mentioned living as a boy in Reading, England, where "Sutton Seeds, Huntley & Palmers' and the *Courage Brewery* were the three names that distinguished the town" (italics added).[3]

Does God still speak to his children? He does. And how? Any way he chooses. And I do love him for that.

If God is always speaking, then why don't we hear? Why do we strain for words from heaven if in fact they have never ceased? And why do we content ourselves with a line to the heart of God that's like a bad cell phone connection—peppered with static and cutting out on every fourth or fifth word? Maybe it's because we're not fully attuned to his voice. We hear what we listen for, after all. Parents are alert to the cries of their children. Teachers recognize the voices of their students. Lovers discern even the softest sigh from their beloved—no words are necessary. More than once Jesus told his followers, "He who has ears to hear, let him hear" (see, for example, Matt. 11:15). He wasn't saying, "Some of you are equipped with two ears and some are not; if you happen to have a pair, now would be the time to use them." He was saying, "Some of you have ears tuned to my voice. Some of you are ready to hear what I have to say. If that's you, it's time to listen up."

Something must happen to our hearts before our ears can be rightly tuned, and that "something" is relationship. "My sheep hear My voice," Jesus said, "and I know them, and they follow Me; and I give eternal life to them, and they will never perish; and no one will snatch them out of My hand" (John 10:27–28). Belonging makes hearing possible. And "belonging" relationships are built on time and trust. I will not hear God well if I am not deliberately, faithfully following him and have not listened long.

If I hadn't glanced up at precisely the right moments of my British adventure, I would have missed "courage." If I had been anticipating another sort of message delivered in a different sort of way, I might have failed to see the word that was doubtless meant for me. As much as I need—and long—to hear from God, I may still miss his voice because of the unexpected content or context of his words. But that does not mean that he is silent. Far from it.

Before man communicated with written words, he drew pictures. Signs before alphabet. Image before language. My first books weren't chapter books—they were picture books. And the pictures conveyed their story as clearly to me as if each page were stuffed with vowels and consonants. God draws too when he has something to say. "The heavens are telling of the glory of God,"

the psalmist writes, "and their expanse is declaring the work of His hands. Day to day pours forth speech, and night to night reveals knowledge. There is no speech, nor are there words; their voice is not heard. Their line has gone out through all the earth, and their utterances to the end of the world" (Ps. 19:1–4).

But like not being able to see the proverbial elephant in the center of the room, we somehow manage to ignore the universe itself as it endlessly testifies on God's behalf. We can't *hear* the forest for the trees any more than we can see it. One evening I was speaking with a man I worked for about the stuff you aren't supposed to discuss with your boss, like "Is there really a God?" He had thought so once, he said, but didn't think so anymore. He shrugged his shoulders and confessed simply, "You prayed the prayer. Something happened to you. I prayed the prayer. Nothing happened to me."

I couldn't let it rest. "Isn't there ever a time," I asked him, "when you think there *might* be a God who cares about us?"

He didn't hesitate. "Sometimes," he said, "when I'm skiing, and I'm at the top of a run, just about to push off—I look around then and I think, *Maybe*." I nodded and waited. He went on. "Or when I put my daughters to bed at night, and they've fallen asleep, and I sit on the floor between their beds and listen to them breathe. I wonder then." But even with God so eloquently speaking, this good man was unconvinced. He was looking for another sort of sound.

I believe, and I can miss it too.

Lying on a hammock strung between two cedars, I gazed heavenward. Texas hill country autumns can be glorious, and this one surely was. I had fled to the country for a few days of solitude and rest, and on this particular afternoon, the hammock had called after a long hike. The wind was cool as it brushed my damp skin, and it whispered in the trees above and around me. Occasionally a deer broke into the clearing and silently gazed my way. Birds flew from limb to limb, calling to one another. I focused on the branches directly above me and then on one small, dangling leaf.

"God," I prayed, "you could tell me you're here by making that one leaf fall. Will you make it fall? Please? I just want to know you're near." I watched and waited. I knew he could send the sign I'd asked for. I thought he might. But he didn't. "Speak, Lord," I think I even prayed. "Your servant is listening." (But obviously not very well.) What I heard next—still focused on the leaf that wasn't falling—was this: "Listen. I *am* speaking. All around you. I'm moving everything that your eye can see and keeping still what's still. There's nothing you can see or touch or smell or hear right now that is not saying my name. And you want to see *one* leaf fall?"

"We live," says writer Ken Gire, "not by bread alone but by every word that proceeds from the mouth of God. Some of those words are spoken at the most unexpected of places that if we're not expecting, we'll miss. Some . . . are spoken by the unlikeliest of people whom we will most likely dismiss if we don't receive them. And some . . . come in the most uncommon of ways that we will react against if we're not accustomed to the unaccustomed ways God speaks."[4]

Giving up our demands opens us to wonder. And the true wonder is that God, however he chooses to speak, is continually offering reassurance, forgiveness, encouragement, rebuke, correction, comfort, hope, and healing with his pictures and with his words.

Aside from our fingerprints, our DNA, the kind of stuff we can't see without fancy, high-tech bifocals, is there anything more distinctive than someone's voice? You and I can change our appearance from day to day, week to week, year to year. But unless we learn the actors' tricks of accent and inflection and mimicry, the voice we're born with is the voice we own. It marks us. It is uniquely ours.

I love the rush of emotion that is triggered in me by a familiar, cherished voice. Just a few words from a family member or a friend can ground me in an instant, helping me to find my place and feel at home. But it is heaven's voice—not theirs—that most often captures my imagination and runs away with it. It is heaven's voice that I want most to hear. How could it not be so?

His is the voice that commanded water to become wine and stilled wild waves and healed withered limbs. The voice that insisted that love trumps law and the brokenhearted are blessed and fishermen can catch men's souls. His is the voice that said, "Follow me," and changed the course of lives forever. The one that made mysterious metaphors for thousands and then explained them to a few. His sweet voice is the voice that comforted friends and even called one of them back from the grave . . . and I suspect that his is the only voice that could compel a man to leave heaven and return to this narrow sliver of reality that we call life.

He said things no one else ever said, in ways that no one else ever will. There was never a time when he wasn't speaking and will never be a time when his voice will not be heard. And as if all this wasn't wonder enough, here's the kicker, the absolute and utterly miraculous truth: It's his voice that speaks truth and comfort and correction and hope to me when I still my heart to listen for it and determine in my mind to obey it.

More than I want to hear from anyone else on this journey, I want to hear from him. His is the voice that has captured and compelled me, that rings with the unmistakable beauty of heaven, and that is as old and familiar as the first voice I must have heard as a child.

One day I will see him. One day I will hear his voice undiluted, undisguised. No message of his will be garbled. No murmur indistinct. Like a sheep that has become fully familiar with his shepherd, I will know God's voice and recognize it. Until then, I will struggle to hear him and to understand him well. My recognition of his lovely voice is mostly after the fact on this side of eternity, but that in no way diminishes my delight in having heard it or dulls my expectant longing to hear it again. *Speak, Lord. Please speak. Your servant really is listening.*

"And he walks with me and he talks with me," the old hymn says, "and tells me I am his own. And the joy we share as we tarry there, none other has ever known." I remember singing those words once and having the friend in the pew next to me lean in and whisper, "No great theology there." I think I may have even nodded. But I hope not. There's enough theology there to keep me attentive for eternity. I don't believe I'll ever exhaust my God's supply of truth-filled words or lose my desire to hear them.

Have you heard the longed-for murmur of heaven lately? Would you like to hear it more clearly? Maybe it's time to cut out some of the static. To drive with the car radio off; to leave the cell phone at home (no, "mute" doesn't count), to ignore the insistent lure of TiVo or Netflix or the nearest cinema multiplex. Maybe it's time to gaze at the heavens or head for the hills, to stop listening for the words you want in the way you want them and open your heart to what—and how—God may be speaking, even now.

"Heaven and earth will pass away, but My words shall not pass away" (Matt. 24:35).

"Now on the last day, the day of the great feast, Jesus stood and cried out, saying, 'If anyone is thirsty, let him come to Me and drink. He who believes in Me, as the Scripture said, "From his innermost being will flow rivers of living water."' . . . So a division occurred in the crowd because of Him. . . . The officers then came to the chief priests and Pharisees, and they said to them, 'Why did you not bring Him?' The officers answered, 'Never has a man spoken the way this man speaks'" (John 7:37–38, 43, 45–46).

"The voice of the LORD is upon the waters; the God of glory thunders, the LORD is over many waters. The voice of the LORD is powerful, the voice of the LORD is majestic. The voice of the LORD breaks the cedars; yes, the LORD breaks in pieces the cedars of Lebanon. . . . The voice of the LORD hews out flames of fire. The voice of the LORD shakes the wilderness; the LORD shakes the wilderness of Kadesh. The voice of the LORD makes the deer to calve and strips the forest bare; and in His temple everything says, 'Glory!'" (Ps. 29:3–5, 7–9).

One Bright Red Bird

The Ache of Hope

Hope is the thing with feathers—
That perches in the soul—
That sings the tune without the words—
And never stops—at all—

Emily Dickinson[1]

"Don't make me hope," I've said to God more than once. "It hurts too much." But hoping is fertile ground, and having hope is much more reasonable than not having it. Especially with a God like ours, whose specialty is nothing less than the impossible.

I always wanted four. For as long as I can remember, I hoped to have four children: two daughters and two sons, spaced evenly through my prime childbearing years like brightly colored dividers in a clean, new notebook. Then a funny thing happened to me on the way to motherhood. I didn't marry young. Somewhere around twenty-seven or so, I began mentally moving the dividers closer to each other. I didn't even marry at thirty. Maybe three would be a fine number after all, I reasoned. Now I've smiled grudgingly at another decade, haven't married yet, and would settle for just one of my long-imagined offspring. The family I used to believe was a certainty is looking more and more like a miscast master plan.

I was just a year away from college when my mother was the same age I am now; my sister's two precious daughters are both teenagers now. Even so, dreams are stubborn things—and although science, logic, and pride might concede that it's time to let them go, the heart does not relent. It holds tight to the very things you coax it to release. I've struggled hard with letting my longed-for children go, because to me they were never only vapor or vain imaginings. These were my babies. They were so real to me that I could almost feel their sweet, smooth skin, smell their wispy hair, and brush their tiny fingers and their toes. I've tried out names for them and scratched my favorites down on tablets: Rebecca and Emily. Emma Lynn. Abigail. Rory and John. Mark, Will, Bryant, and Andrew.

Because no one has shared their name with me, I have not handed out these names I've long imagined. Because no one has called me wife or mother, I've instead become Aunt Leigh. To my nieces, Katharine and Victoria, I'm a sort of "Mom Light," a cross between Glinda the Good Witch and their fairy-godmother-in-the-wings. They are my two favorite girls on the planet, and I love them desperately—but they are not mine. They are my sister's daughters, although she has shared them with me from the day they each were born—a mighty gift, and one I don't belittle. I am grateful beyond words to have watched them grow. Friends too have honored me as "aunt," and so to Katie, Robert, Caitlin, Nathan, Jack, and Abbigayle, I'm an "aunt" by kind appointment, a treasured title generously bestowed with each new little one's arrival.

I wish I could say it's been enough. I wish I could say the longing is gone or that I'm fine with the possibility of permanent childlessness. But that would be a lie. My head turns involuntarily in the direction of strollers the way a man's might when a tall, attractive blonde walks past, and a trip to Baby Gap to buy a shower gift can render me frog-throated and misty-eyed in minutes. I'm held fast in this embarrassing longing, and I don't know if I'll be released—or when. I've managed to keep my options open when the easiest thing would have been to give in and give up, and I do believe it could still happen. But according to the experts, it probably won't be in the "usual" way.

Leave it to the news magazines to offer a dream an editorially assisted suicide. Some people's hopes are derailed in a hospital room or a boardroom or a courtroom; mine have been assaulted more than once in the checkout line at the grocery store. It was there I learned I was more likely to be killed by a terrorist than married after forty (news that came, thankfully, before I reached that milestone), and now I am hit with another blow: "Babies vs. Career: The Harsh Facts about Fertility." It seems, according to *Time* magazine, that only 0.1 percent of babies in the United

States are born to women forty-five or older, and that at forty-two, 90 percent of a woman's eggs are abnormal and she has only a 7.8 percent chance of giving birth without serious scientific intervention. And what about those "Hollywood moms" who are having beautifully perfect babies well into their forties? Donor eggs, *Time* tactlessly reveals.[2]

It seems that twenty-seven is the age at which a woman's chance of getting pregnant begins to decline. (Did my body send my heart a coded message when I adjusted my expectations at just that age?) And nature randomly self-selects when we don't police our bodies on our own: at twenty, the risk of miscarriage is about 9 percent; it doubles by thirty-five and then doubles again by the time a woman reaches forty.

Believe me, I've done the math. Should God in his goodness bring me a husband tomorrow, and should I beat the odds and conceive almost immediately—even then I'd be on the wrong side of the rough in nine months' time. Hope is getting harder and harder to come by.

I've noticed that my family and friends don't speak of children as a given for me anymore. Hardly anyone says casually in conversation, "You'll see when you have kids of your own." A family of my own has become not only my personal, against-the-odds longing but also my intensely private one.

Even so, I am frequently caught in the crossfire of the inevitable kid conversations that spring up among women my age. If they do happen to realize I'm the odd one out, they usually offer uncomfortable platitudes, which sound polite but which in my heart I imagine must be accompanied by either smug superiority or quiet pity—or both.

"But you've got so much free time," they say. Or, "At least your living room is not ankle-deep in toys." These things are mostly true too—but I've never seen them as the enviable consolation prizes of childlessness. I'm not even sure that I should.

As strange as it may sound, in my completely unwilling failure to reproduce, I don't feel less womanly. Every year that passes finds me feeling more feminine, more nurturing, deeper, wiser, fuller, and more free. Here's an unexpected little paradox: While the likelihood that I will give birth dwindles, the hope that I will give life does not. It grows stronger by the day.

I realize I'm not the only one whose dreams have been seriously delayed. I understand there are things far more threatening and frightening and sad than being without a husband and children. But this has long been my desire, and so it is the place from which I can truthfully speak. I know others who have had the very things I long for, then seen them wrenched away by tragedy or selfishness or simple neglect. I know that some pray for cancer to be gone, or for still limbs to stretch and move, or for the hardened heart of another to melt, or to hear that they're finally forgiven. My heart goes out to them. I want them to keep on hoping too. I do.

It would be easier to let hope quietly die, but I don't. I choose to keep the faith because, in a way I can't completely fathom, I know that faith is the truest substructure of the things for which we hope—the real, actual foundation and substance of the heart's fiercest longing. It's the required "deposit" that must precede any future blessing. But even though I accept that an unbreakable connection exists between believing and receiving, it's easier for me to believe for another's hope than for my own.

A special place in the heart of the hills has become a refuge for me, and I go there with the expectation that God himself will greet me. He has not failed me yet.

The foreman's home sits across a cattle guard, down a gravel road, into a canyon that the wind whispers through, and beyond a rock riverbed. Each time I arrive, he bundles my bags and drives me to my final stop.

The Quiet House is small and sparely furnished. There is a sitting room with a soot-marked stone fireplace rising up to a beamed ceiling where a tiny loft is tucked. The kitchen is basic, with one small table, four chairs, and a cushioned window seat. A double bed with a chenille coverlet joins the two rooms, and the tiny bathroom off a tight hallway leads out to a porch swing and a neatly stacked woodpile.

The house's furnishings are comfortable and calming, but they are not fine. Two gently worn armchairs and an ottoman face the fireplace, and an antique Bible lies open on the side table under a window. A small desk and chair stand nearby, and the second right-hand drawer of the desk stores a stack of spiral-bound stenographer's pads. The house's previous guests have journaled their thoughts in these notebooks, and my entries blend with theirs in a kind of real-life *Pilgrim's Progress* that I read each time I come.

In a closet off the sitting room a hammock lies folded, ready to string between the two tallest cedars out front, and a big bin of corn waits to offer to the only other guests I'll see while I am there: the deer, javelinas, skunks, raccoons, turkeys, possums, and squirrels who steal up in the yard at night and forage for the food they've come to expect. The birds gather too and feast above the heads of the other animals if the squirrels have not arrived first and hung upside down to steal the seed from the feeders.

Here is a special kind of bliss: passing a silent night with a crackling fire in the fireplace, the rooms lit with oil lamps, and me alone in the kitchen with a steaming cup of tea, watching the parade of wildlife in front of the big bay window. No phone, no radio, no television. Just me and the curious kingdom-dwellers beyond the window glass, peacefully coexisting in plain sight of one another.

On a recent trip there, I wrote these words in my own journal and did not leave them behind:

> How is it possible to long for something so deeply and so desperately and never see it? Haven't I trusted in You, God, or have I only not trusted in me? Is the desire of my heart from You? And if so—haven't You promised to give it when I delight myself in You? And haven't I done that? Then what? When? How? I have waited on You alone. I want You, and no one else, to give me my desire of a husband and a family.
>
> Did Sarah ever remind You of her age? This Saturday, Lord God, is my birthday. Another year and my desire is the same as it has ever been. All my distractions and old allegiances are gone. Killed. Severed. I am no one's now but Yours.
>
> I need You to give me the desires of my heart. I cannot get them for myself, by myself. Help me to look expectantly to the future You are forging for me, even now. To believe Your good loving-kindness exists for me and not just for others. Help me to count on You, to hope in You with confident assurance. Please. It's midnight, and I'm here: begging for my bread before the only one who can give it. Prepare a banquet for me, just because You are good. Please God, would You do that for me?

The next morning, just after sunrise, I sat at the table again, looking out at the empty yard, stark and bare in late December. The trees had long since shed their leaves, and the scene played in a decidedly monochromatic tone: everything as far as I could see was gray, or brown, or umber—flat and faded like an old photograph. The view was utterly colorless . . . until one bright red bird fluttered in and perched on a distant limb.

In this context, he was more than obvious—he was outrageous. Even his beak was red. He stood out with no effort on his part; he couldn't help himself. My eyes were riveted to him, willing him to stay and not fly off with the only glimpse of vibrant color for miles. And he did stay. As I watched him, I thought of the little girl in the red coat who wandered through a throng of black-and-white-hued adults in *Schindler's List*. His appearance was that vivid, that strange.

My feathered friend was a glimpse of pure hope on a cold winter scrim. My dreams were still out of sight, but this one bright red bird looked for all the world like a deposit of brilliant faith in a bland sky, and I could hardly write for looking at him. His bold color seemed almost as ridiculous as the hope of a forty-year-old woman for a family of her own. But he was there—and he flew! The God who made him and slipped him into my sight line at that moment was and is the very One to whom my hope should fly: my strength, my song, my salvation, and the giver of every good thing.

My lingering longing for a husband and children has caused me to wonder: Does a husband make a woman into a wife? Does the birth of a child make her a mother? What lies sleeping inside a daughter of Eve that waits to be called out by one or the other or both? Is it hidden there all along, or does it only compose itself when a specific beloved calls it forth? What about those married women who close their hearts to their husbands and refuse to love because they do not feel well loved? What about the parents who abandon their children outright or withhold their affection unless they consistently see demonstrated the kind of behavior their rigid standards require?

Could a mother's love also lurk inside the heart of a woman who nurtures a stubborn garden, or a book, or a classroom of other people's children? Is it mother-love to cheer the efforts of an awkward teenager's attempt to serve a volleyball, or to set a perfect table and prepare a favorite meal (whether it's hot dogs or homemade pasta) for a dear friend's birthday? To craft a poem or tell a story that will delight a small handful of people, or even just one? Couldn't that be a kind of mother-love too?

Does a wife's heart beat in the woman who believes resolutely in someone else's dream when the rest of the world says "get serious"? Who listens for the meaning behind the words "I'm tired" or "I'd rather not talk about it, that's all"? Is it wife-love to overlook an unthinking slight or to remember that someone else likes chewy cookies best, instead of the crispy ones that you prefer? To stay still and let the silence speak when words can't say enough?

Maybe the same kind of love is there for the spending whether it's focused on one man, or four children, or a roomful of old friends, or a stranger. Maybe it's not lost in the spending, either, but strengthened and sharpened and multiplied.

I do wish I had someone who had promised to stay with me until death parts us. I wish I tucked our children into bed at night. I wish we could grow older in full view of one another and laugh at secrets no one else would know. But if I had all those longed-for things, would I be fully given over to them?

Can I reasonably expect to keep my heart all to myself, then hand it over in an instant at a candlelit altar or in a brightly lit delivery room? Probably not. More likely the work will have to start before then. And shouldn't it start now, today, believing in faith that a wife's heart can love before it sees her husband and that a mother's heart can nurture before it holds her child? "Choose hope," a good friend of mine once said. "It's entirely reasonable." She knows Jesus. She may be right.

Should I continue to hope that God will bring me to a man who adores God and adores me too? To hope that this same man might be sure enough of us both that he is unafraid to choose a single road instead of two? To think that our love might both glorify our heavenly Father and deeply satisfy us? To trust that there could still be room for the children I can't stop dreaming of, however they might come? Why not? O God, why not? *"He who did not spare His own Son, but delivered Him over for us all, how will He not also with Him freely give us all things?"* (Rom. 8:32).

Was the cardinal embarrassed by the blatant audacity of his bloodred feathers? No, he was not—not in the least. So why do I dress my longing down, ashamed to hold fast to it as another year goes by? Why do I pretend it doesn't matter anymore? Why *shouldn't* I hope outrageously in my good God, with or without a bright red bird in sight? His loving-kindness is everlasting, and so in faith I do believe. May he help my unbelief and—until that day—make me strong enough to embrace the ache I am still too hopeful and hungry to quietly put away.

"Hope is the thing with feathers—" wrote poet Emily Dickinson, *"that perches on the soul—that sings the tune without the words—and never stops—at all—"* My bright red bird seemed to echo those words to me. Some hopes just won't stop singing, no matter how far-fetched or impossible they seem. You don't inhabit them; they inhabit you. And maybe it's good that they do.

What hope is stretching your heart these days? The hope for a prodigal to return home? For a hard heart to melt? For forgiveness to be extended and an old, ugly wound to heal? Can you see hope not as a desolate outpost on the way to fulfillment but as a worthy lingering place in itself? Are you willing to receive the instruction that comes on the feathered wings of hope? If not, are you willing to be made willing?

"For nothing will be impossible with God" (Luke 1:37).

"But as for me, I will watch expectantly for the LORD; I will wait for the God of my salvation. My God will hear me" (Micah 7:7).

"Now faith is the assurance of things hoped for, the conviction of things not seen. For by it the men of old gained approval. By faith we understand that the worlds were prepared by the word of God, so that what is seen was not made out of things which are visible. . . . And without faith it is impossible to please Him, for he who comes to God must believe that He is and that He is a rewarder of those who seek Him" (Heb. 11:1–2, 6).

Faith and Falling

The Ache of Trusting

'Tis so sweet to trust in Jesus;
Just to take Him at His word;
Just to rest upon His promise;
Just to know, "Thus saith the Lord."

Louisa M. R. Stead

There's no ache quite like the ache of uncertainty. We feel most empowered by knowledge, by the solid assurance that something is undoubtedly so. To be sure—utterly, resolutely sure about anything—is to possess a distinct and strong advantage. Or is it?

The most exhilarating, enlightening trip I've ever taken lasted less than ten minutes from start to finish. I wasn't carrying my driver's license, my passport, or my keys. My traveling companion on this brief journey was a man I'd just met, and I quite literally trusted him with my life. He'd been married three times, he told me, and he sported more tattoos and body piercings than it would have been polite to count. His name was Tom.

Tom and I quickly bonded on a beautiful January day in the cold, clear skies over South Texas. Less than two hours after we met, we leaped from an airplane together at 13,000 feet, hooked back-to-front at four points by metal harnesses. He was in charge of our parachute. My only job was falling. We both did just fine.

The jump was a birthday gift from four good friends who'd heard me say more than once that I wanted to skydive and did me the honor of taking me at my word. On the day of the jump, we drove to a small rural airport where I watched a terrifying video, signed an even more terrifying waiver, changed into a borrowed jumpsuit, received a leather helmet and goggles, and took an hour or so of instruction. (Considering the event at hand, I'd never felt—or been—more unprepared in my life.)

As Tom and I boarded the small prop plane with the other "divers"—some experienced solo jumpers and the rest rookie, tandem jumpers like me—my enabling friends settled into their lawn chairs near the hangar. The plane climbed, and as it did, the noise of the propellers made hearing nearly impossible. I kept waiting for cold fear to send my stomach plummeting to my ankles. But even as Tom and I commando-crept forward and crouched at the open door, that paralyzing fear never came—only the kind of butterflies that used to accompany exam day or a long-anticipated first date.

We would rock forward twice, Tom had explained, and on our third rock we would tumble into the open sky, my arms folded across my chest. When I felt his tap on my shoulder, I could extend my arms under his. It occurred to me then that Tom hadn't said what I was supposed to do when it was time for us to land.

"What about the landing?" I shouted against the rushing wind.

"We'll talk on the way down," he shouted back, "after I pull the chute."

"After I pull the chute" seemed like an odd time to rehearse such a mission-critical maneuver, but who was I to say? I'd never done this before, and Tom had, hundreds of times. He reached around my shoulder to give me an encouraging "thumbs-up," and then we rocked once, twice, and fell . . . gloriously . . . surrounded by nothing but sky.

The jump was everything I had hoped it would be and more. The view was incredible, and the feeling of being carried along on an invisible current was pure bliss. I loved every second of it. While I was less than thrilled about Tom's decision to talk me through the landing on the way down, in retrospect he was quite right. The time for tutoring was not prejump (when my head was filled with so many other details that I would have likely forgotten most of it), and conversation would have been impossible during our free-falling descent. He instructed me when I was least distracted and most euphoric: as we floated under our billowing chute to the firm, familiar ground below.

For days afterward I puzzled at the fact that the awful fear I had expected to materialize never did. At the plane's open doorway, poised to fall, only one clear thought had come to mind:

I've been here before. No, I'd never skydived. I wasn't sure about *it.* But I *had* been perched on the brink of something untried and uncertain more than once. And each time, the arms I'd trusted to hold me had done so.

"Daddy's got you" were the words that made possible almost every one of my childhood leaps of faith. Standing poolside at age four or maybe five, ten toes gripping the edge and ten yearning fingertips outstretched, "Daddy's got you" were the words that plunged me into the deep end and into his waiting arms. I wasn't sure of the water. I wasn't sure of my ability to stay afloat. I wasn't sure of what would happen after my tiny feet left the warm pavement . . . but I was very sure of him.

This magic phrase also proved useful when the training wheels were removed from my bicycle for the first time and I was sent wobbling down the driveway, unbalanced and afraid. Dad held on until he was sure I was steady—but not as long as I thought he had. I was already pedaling on my own when I believed he was still holding me up, and it somehow worked better that way.

There was then—and is now—little more exhilarating than venturing out with no better option than to trust and then finding the object of my trust worthy of it. "Now faith," said the writer of the book of Hebrews, "is the assurance of things hoped for, the conviction of things not seen" (Heb. 11:1). In other words, faith is the choice to perceive as fact what is not readily evident to my senses—and trust is the testing of that perception in some concrete way. What skydiving, swimming, and riding a bicycle unaided all had in common was this: Each act physically manifested my inward belief that I would be caught and cared for. In none of these instances had I depended solely upon myself. In fact, in each of them I attempted something I was quite certain was *beyond* myself. And in each case the act of trusting forged a strong and powerful memory of the kind of grand adventure that comes only from letting go.

My father, who more than once made me brave, did the bravest thing of all himself the year I turned thirteen. On that birthday he wrote me a letter (delivered with one long-stemmed red rose) that celebrated my short life with typical paternal enthusiasm but ended with quite daring words that went something like this: "Your mother and I will always be proud of you, but it is your Maker you must answer to and yourself you will face in the mirror each day. Many things may change, but this one will remain constant: your dad's love for his daughter."

Early on, my dad trusted me to another. He set me free from pleasing him to fully follow the One most deserving of my trust: Jesus. The dreams I was encouraged to follow were God's dreams for me—never someone else's. Maybe that's why, in the days since, I have thrilled to trust and prove bold words like these from my heavenly Father's book: "Who will separate us from the love of Christ? Will tribulation, or distress, or persecution, or famine, or nakedness, or peril, or sword? . . . For I am convinced that neither death, nor life, nor angels, nor principalities, nor things present, nor things to come, nor powers, nor height, nor depth, nor any other created thing, will be able to separate us from the love of God, which is in Christ Jesus our Lord" (Rom. 8:35, 38–39).

These very tangible forces test and try us; they threaten our faith and boldly demand that we prove it by trusting. Like the dying boy's father who begged Jesus to heal his son, then confessed, "I do believe; help my unbelief" (Mark 9:24), we stand in our critical moments sure but not utterly certain. Believing and yet still doubtful. But each time we move, each time we venture forward, anxious but determined to trust, we witness a small sliver of God's kingdom come, "on earth, as it is in heaven." Moments of trust are incarnational moments, whether we realize them as such or not.

My wildest leaps of faith seem utterly insignificant compared to this one: a simple virgin is visited by an angel and told she will become pregnant with a child whose father is God. Nothing in her frame of reference could have prepared her for such a pronouncement. Nothing could have prepared *anyone* (save a lunatic) for such a pronouncement. It defied logic. It ignored the precepts of biology. It slapped the face of culture and propriety. The angel's words ushered in what poet Madeleine L'Engle has called "the irrational season; where love blooms bright and wild," insisting that "had Mary been filled with reason, there'd have been no room for the child."[1] I love that.

My favorite depiction of this stunning encounter is Botticelli's painting *The Annunciation*. In it a beautiful, winged angel stoops low before a demure and graceful Mary—both she and the angel bathed in rich, warm color and shaped with flowing lines. Their soft receptiveness is contrasted by the angular context in which they are placed: a geometric foreground of straight lines and hard edges, broken by a stark, gray portico behind. In the center of that portico, a single tree (foreshadowing, perhaps?) stands straight and solitary against the cloudless sky. Winsome openness is clearly juxtaposed against hard reason in the artist's rendering, as surely as it must have been that fateful day. After all, virgins don't become pregnant by an unseen power; ordinary girls don't give birth to God. Kings don't come from commoners, and angels don't do birth announcements.

Luke reports that Mary was somewhat troubled by the angel's appearing, but not to the point of resisting the life-altering news he bore: "You will conceive in your womb," the heavenly messenger told her, "and bear a son, and you shall name Him Jesus. He will be great and will be called the Son of the Most High; and the Lord God will give Him the throne of His father David; and

He will reign over the house of Jacob forever; and His kingdom will have no end" (Luke 1:31–33). Hearing this and clearly understanding "where babies come from," the gentle mother-to-be had just one question: "How can this be, since I am a virgin?"

Once she heard the angel's explanation that her child would be supernaturally conceived, she simply answered: "Behold, the bondslave of the Lord; be it done to me according to your word" (Luke 1:38). I marvel at that kind of trust. But it didn't stop there. Mary said yes to the moment of conception, irrational and wild as it was. Then for months, in the face of confusion and scorn, she kept on saying yes. God may have supernaturally announced her miracle baby—but he didn't supernaturally deliver him. He came the old-fashioned way, after nine months of gestation and then hours of excruciating labor. Her act of trust was not quickly made and then forgotten. She lived in the space of her faith-filled words ("May it be done to me . . .") far longer than I have ever been required to.

Mary faithfully received the words of the angel and just as trustingly received "the Word implanted" that was able to save her soul and mine. And her one sustained "yes" brought his sweet kingdom closer than it had ever been before. Trusting does that every time.

Writer Brennan Manning has called "our need for an unfaltering trust in the love of God . . . the most urgent need we have."[2] The angel's stunning pronouncement to the would-be mother of Christ was preceded by the assurance of a loving, present God: "Greetings, favored one! The Lord is with you" (Luke 1:28). My earthly father's assurance that "your dad's love for his daughter" would never change was what I needed to venture into strange territory unhobbled by fear. Knowing we are loved makes us brave. "Perfect love," said the apostle John, "casts out fear" (1 John 4:18).

If Mary had doubted that God meant to do good both to and through her, she might not have answered as she did. But she didn't trust the plan—she trusted the One who made the plan. She couldn't see the future, but with her eyes of faith she could see the One who shaped it. Her steadfast assurance of God's love compelled her to relinquish control of her very body to a preposterous idea, but God opened her heart long before he invaded her womb. She confessed her frailty and admitted that she was the recipient of power ("May it be done to me . . .") but not its source. She took the free fall of faith because she was already a woman in love.

I've only been to the circus once in my life, and I remember only one moment from it. The moment that has remained fixed in my brain does not involve animals or clowns or cotton candy. Instead, it is a moment of vacant space and the sound of a collective "aaahhhh." It is the moment of emptiness between an acrobat's release of one trapeze bar and the swinging catch of another. Arms outstretched, the artist flings himself from safety into danger and is rescued from danger to safety again. It is a beautiful space, that in-between space he briefly inhabits. And the crowd senses it, gasping as one when he enters it.

I couldn't have known it then, but the ache of that uncertain moment would present itself over and over again in ordinary and extraordinary situations. At 13,000 feet over a patchwork earth and in the seconds before a first kiss. Between the words "I'm so sorry" and the hoped-for "It's all right." After a frightening diagnosis but well before its grateful cure. After a heart-wrenching question but preceding its reassuring answer. Between "Will you?" and "I will." Between "I love you" and "I love you too." Such in-between spaces are incredibly lonely, inhabitable only for the one who believes he is deeply loved beyond whatever outcome he may see.

The small enclosure lay past the city gate north of the temple and across the valley known as the Kidron. Locals called the place Gethsemane, a name that meant "oil press," and some say it was a tiny fruit and olive garden near an olive press. Perhaps only seventy feet square (no larger than a sprawling suburban yard today), it was a favored retreat—a quiet resting place for prayer or sleep or both. On the night before Jesus's death, after he had broken bread with his disciples and sent one of them away to betray him, Jesus gathered there with the remaining eleven. He quoted to them the words of the prophet Zechariah, saying, "You will all fall away because of Me this night, for it is written, 'I will strike down the shepherd, and the sheep of the flock shall be scattered'" (Matt. 26:31).

Gesturing to eight of the eleven, he asked them to sit and wait for him while he went farther into the enclosure to pray, taking with him Peter, James, and John. "My soul is deeply grieved to the point of death," he confided, "remain here and keep watch with Me" (Matt. 26:38). Taking a few more steps, he fell on his face and called out to God, "My Father, if it is possible, let this cup pass from Me; yet not as I will, but as You will" (v. 39). Returning to his friends, he found them sleeping and asked them again to watch and pray. Then he beseeched his Father again, saying, "My Father, if this cannot pass away unless I drink it, Your will be done" (v. 42).

Jesus knew his Father could remove the cup of suffering from him; he also knew the Father very likely would not. The decision would belong to God. Like his human mother had done thirty-three years before, Jesus deliberately surrendered the choice to another. How similar his words were to hers! Luke's Gospel records that he prayed so fervently and desperately that his sweat became bloody as it fell to the ground. Three times he prayed. Three times he returned to his dearest friends and found them sleeping. An angel came from heaven and strengthened him, but the cup was not removed. He would drink it to the dregs. As Alfred Edersheim said, "It was the Christ undergoing Death by man and for man; the Incarnate God, the God-Man, submitting Himself vicariously to the deepest humiliation, and paying the utmost penalty: Death—all Death."[3]

Knowing with certainty he was loved by the Father, Jesus gave himself up to the Father's plan. Thursday he prayed. Friday he suffered and died and was buried. Between Friday and Sunday an empty space—a terrible pause—ensued. He had "let go" of this life, trusting his Father's loving plan. But on Sunday morning, he firmly grasped eternal life, having won it for himself and for us. "For the death that He died, He died to sin once for all; but the life that He lives, He lives to God" (Rom. 6:10).

Even Jesus was not exempt from trusting. Even the Son of God placed himself into the hands of the Father, not seizing control for himself but relinquishing it fully to God. And those trusting moments brought his kingdom closer still. How, then, can I expect to escape the same surrender . . . and why would I want to try?

I am not always comfortable when I am called on to trust. I am not always graceful about leaping in faith into his waiting arms. But I am compelled by love to try . . . and to let go by grace of what I know and can see, so that I can apprehend by faith what I have not yet seen but do believe. The words of an old hymn ring true for me: *"Jesus, Jesus, how I trust Him! How I've proved Him o'er and o'er. Jesus, Jesus, precious Jesus, oh for grace to trust Him more!"*

A poster in my old college dorm room proclaimed: "A ship in the harbor is safe . . . but that is not what ships are made for. Trust the unseen wind." It seemed easier then. Less was riding on the exercise

of trust when I was twenty-one. My failure to do so then was more easily disguised. But these days I live out in the open. I speak of trust. I write about it (a fact I'm often reminded of when I fail to exercise it). I do believe. And at times, I need the One I believe to help my unbelief. I am so grateful that in his great mercy, he does.

If God has placed you in a moment that requires trust—or the long sustaining of it—he has brought you to a place of great intimacy and possibility. Trust is for lovers, not for strangers. So instead of asking, "Do I dare?" why not ask instead, "Am I loved?" If the answer is yes, then trust is the only reasonable response. As you and I wait in faith, trusting God to work or heal or help or deliver or strengthen, we enter a space into which the kingdom may come. Words like "Be it done to me according to your will," and "Not what I will, but what you will" are just the sort of invitation our good King waits to hear.

"From my distress I called upon the LORD; the LORD answered me and set me up in a large place. The LORD is for me; I will not fear; what can man do to me? The LORD is for me among those who help me; therefore I shall look with satisfaction on those who hate me. It is better to take refuge in the LORD than to trust in man. It is better to take refuge in the LORD than to trust in princes" (Ps. 118:5–9).

"Now faith is the assurance of things hoped for, the conviction of things not seen. For by it men of old gained approval. By faith we understand that the worlds were prepared by the word of God, so that what is seen was not made out of things which are visible. . . . And without faith it is impossible to please Him, for he who comes to God must believe that He is and that He is a rewarder of those who seek Him" (Heb. 11:1–3, 6).

"Come, let us return to the LORD. For He has torn us, but He will heal us; He has wounded us, but He will bandage us. He will revive us after two days; He will raise us up on the third day, that we may live before Him. So let us know, let us press on to know the LORD. His going forth is as certain as the dawn; and He will come to us like the rain, like the spring rain watering the earth" (Hosea 6:1–3).

"Gimme Some Sugar"

The Ache for Healing

The hands of the King are the hands of a healer.

J. R. R. Tolkien, *The Return of the King*

Sickness has gotten an awfully bad rap. There's even a rumor afoot that God-followers with enough faith need never suffer illness at all—or if they do, their infirmity shouldn't be final or fatal. Medicine now routinely performs in what was once the exclusive territory of miracles . . . and even aging's effects can be diligently and artfully disguised. But all around us . . . people do still suffer. And not everyone who pleads for healing, on this side of heaven, receives it.

*M*y good friend's hospital room seemed warm—very warm—yet he lay buried up to his ears in sterile cotton blankets. I had taken only a few steps inside when I noticed that his narrow shoulders were shaking. "Hey, Boo," I whispered. "Are you *cold*?" As he shook his head no, I could see that he wasn't shivering at all—he was crying. A tape player sat on his bedside tray, but the tape he had been listening to was stopped.

"What's wrong?" I asked. "Did something happen to upset you?"

As his eyes met mine his words came out in a rush. "That lady on the tape said she had cancer, but she prayed in faith and God healed her. I've been praying too, and God hasn't healed me. I'm just getting worse and worse. What's the matter? Doesn't he love me too? Is my faith too weak for him to heal me? What am I doing wrong?"

He was thirty years old, and AIDS was wreaking havoc on his young body. God had plucked him from a life of destruction and despair and given him a tender new heart, but his outer man was wasted and frail, and he was growing weaker by the day. I extricated the tape from the tape player and buried it in my purse. "Let's not listen to this anymore today," I said. "I don't *know* why God healed her and hasn't healed you. I've prayed for that too. But I do know he loves you and that he can't mean for you to compare yourself to someone else . . . or your situation to theirs."

He wiped his moist brown eyes and swallowed, but not easily, for his mouth was parched and dry. He tried to turn over on his

127

back, but the simple effort made him wince. His skin was hot to the touch. "Does God want me to be sick?" he asked again, finally situated. "Do you think he means for me to die? The lady said it was never his will for his children to suffer or be victims . . . so how can this be happening? What am I doing wrong?"

The pain of my friend's illness was wretched enough—but the pain of wondering where his merciful God might be in the midst of it was surely a thousand times worse. I wanted to yank the tape some well-meaning friend must have given him out of its hard plastic shell, foot by foot, and then fling the whole unthreaded mess out the window. But more than that, I wanted my sweet friend to have comfort, and peace, and a steady, firm hope in his God's goodness. I understood his questions. But whatever answers I might have mustered in that moment would not have been enough. He just wanted to get better . . . and in spite of his faith, he wasn't.

Job was the good man's name, and his rep was golden: "blameless, upright, fearing God, and turning away from evil" (Job 1:1). If not for a conversation between two age-old adversaries, Job might have sailed smoothly through his blessed life. But one day God said to Satan, "Have you seen my servant Job?" and the test was on. "Touch all that he has," Satan posited, and "he will surely curse You to Your face" (Job 1:11). Mysteriously, God gave Satan permission to do just that, sparing Job his own life and limb but ensuring nothing more than that.

Job's livestock and servants were slaughtered. Fire from heaven consumed them. His ten sons and daughters were killed when their house fell in on them. Everything he possessed was wiped away in a single day. When the awful news came, Job tore his robe, shaved his head, and said, "Naked I came from my mother's womb, and naked I shall return there. The LORD gave and the LORD has taken away. Blessed be the name of the LORD" (Job 1:21).

A second conversation between God and Satan ensued, and this time God removed the ban on Job's body—giving Satan leave to strike Job with sickness. And he did, afflicting him with "sore boils from the sole of his foot to the crown of his head" (Job 2:7). His wife suggested Job curse God and die, effectively putting himself out of his misery. Job declined, asking her instead, "Shall we indeed accept good from God and not accept adversity?" (Job 2:10). Then his friends surrounded and not-so-helpfully interrogated him, questioning his own integrity and insisting that he must be hiding some secret sin.

He wasn't. He was nothing more or less than a good man who had suffered great loss. And although those losses would ultimately be restored, no explanation for them was ever offered. Job never knew why. And it was God's providence, not Job's own goodness or lack of it, that both allowed him to fall sick and caused him to be well.

If I ran the world, the righteous wouldn't suffer. Children wouldn't die. Awful accidents wouldn't happen, and disease wouldn't win. Ever. But God, not me, reigns sovereign over the affairs of men. I would arrange things so that no one need ever ask "Why?" But in God's design, "Why?" is a question never far from human hearts and lips . . . and one that is not answered on demand. "I shall know why—" poet Emily Dickinson wrote, "when Time is over—/and I have ceased to wonder why—/ Christ will explain each separate anguish/in the fair schoolroom of the sky."[1]

It is a fact that not everyone who wants healing gets it. Not everyone who begs for deliverance will be delivered. Not everyone who aches for wellness is made well. My friend with AIDS wasn't. He died at thirty. Another dear friend of mine died just days after his forty-sixth birthday—a good man who loved

God and served him with everything he had. But that didn't make him immune to sickness or guarantee him healing when sickness came.

Even after standing beside the graves of these two dear ones and others whose sicknesses claimed them far too soon, I confess I do still believe in miraculous healing. I believe in asking for it, and I believe God does grant it. But I've not seen a cause-and-effect equation that delivers it without fail if we only pull the right levers and press the right buttons. Jesus himself seldom healed in the same manner twice. Candidates for his healing touch were as different from one another as they could be: a centurion's son with a fever is healed "in absentia"; so is a woman's daughter who suffers from "an unclean spirit." But a woman who touches the hem of Jesus's garment is also healed, although she never asks him to make her well. A deaf man receives back his hearing when the Son of God places his fingers in the man's ears and touches his tongue with saliva; a blind man's eyes are plastered with mud and spit, and he sees. A man who has waited thirty-eight years beside the same pool for the stirring of the waters is seen by Jesus and healed *without* the water being stirred—but first he is asked if wants to be made well, as if his desire were not obvious! All of these were healed with no recognizable pattern, yet one of Jesus's most passionate, committed followers—the apostle Paul—prayed over and over for healing from an unnamed ailment, and healing never came. He's hard to pin down, our God, and impossible to "manage." And something tells me he would have it no other way.

Our desire for healing holds a special tension: If we believe that God is powerful, if we believe in his ability to heal, what do we do with the uncertainty of whether or not he *will*? And if he does not heal when healing is desired, should we construe that as a reflection of his diminished love or power, an indication that something is not right with us, or simply a reality to be dealt with—nothing more? It's that *"Will you?"* gap that gets us—the aching, vacant space between what we believe God *can* do for anyone and what we hope he *will* do for us.

The leper in Matthew 8 came to Jesus, bowed low before him, and proclaimed, "Lord, if You are willing, You can make me clean" (v. 2). His request came in the form of a statement. He believed the Son of God had healing power, but he did not know whether it was Jesus's will to heal him in that moment. So he simply said as much as he knew . . . and left the rest to Jesus. He put himself in a position to receive healing, seeking the One who could effect it, and he professed his belief that healing was possible. Then he waited to see if it would apply in his case.

Just as the leper broke the taboos of his culture to approach the teacher, the teacher broke the constraints of Jewish law to minister to the sick man: "Jesus stretched out His hand and touched him, saying, 'I am willing; be cleansed.' And immediately his leprosy was cleansed" (v. 3). It seems that in this case, at this moment, Jesus was indeed willing to heal. But if he had *not* healed the leper in that moment, he would have been no less the Son of God and no less good. And the leper would have been no less right to offer his request to Jesus in faith, even if the outcome had not been full and immediate healing.

"God's goal for His people in this age," writes pastor John Piper, "is not primarily to rid them of sickness and pain but to purge us of all the remnants of sin and cause us in our weakness to cleave to Him as our only hope."[2] If there is any common thread among the healing stories of Jesus, this is it: Needy people placed themselves before him, believing that he could heal them and hoping that he would. So we too must willingly place ourselves before him, like the leper did, and see him as our best hope. "It is fitting that a child ask his father for relief in trouble," says

Piper. "And it is fitting that a loving Father give His child only what is best. And that He *always* does: sometimes healing now, sometimes not. But always, always, what is best for us."[3]

"Sometimes healing now, sometimes not" is a hard, hard place to live. It's a mighty struggle to remain weak and yet hopeful before a God who could change everything if he only would. And it's a glorious thing to behold when someone does it well. My friend Charlie struggled with an awful sickness for a year or more before he died. I have no doubt he wanted to be healed. I know for certain that he and many others prayed for that healing. It was not completed before his death, but the evidence of it, even during his suffering, was strong and unmistakable.

My friend and I served together on a large church staff for several years. A quiet servant, a caring manager, and a gifted musician, he was adept at making things happen, at setting the stage, whether for worship or for a meeting, for fellowship or for service. He felt most comfortable behind the scenes, though, and much less so in front. His heart was kind, and his quiet steadiness provided support for many—but he was also an intensely private person, perhaps even a little shy. As a never-married bachelor, Charlie did not always seem at ease with the inevitable awkwardness of interpersonal relationships, but many loved and treasured him, including me.

His illness progressed slowly but steadily, and after a time he could no longer work. Those of us who were accustomed to seeing him each day missed him terribly. We spoke on the phone, and when we did, I expressed my desire to get together. "Aw, Leigh," he'd say, "I look so bad I'd scare you." Try as I might, I couldn't get him to relent. But one evening when we were about to hang up the phone, I said again, "Charlie, I sure would like to see you," and this time, to my surprise, he suggested an outing with two other friends of ours for that weekend. "Y'all could come by here and we could go to dinner," he offered. "Then if I'm still feeling okay, maybe we could take in a movie."

When Friday came, I was the first to arrive. Charlie had left a yellow sticky note on the door of his apartment that said, "Open. Come on up." When I reached the top of the stairs he came out from his bedroom, and I tried hard not to blink. In the few months since I'd last seen him, he must have lost 60 to 75 pounds. He looked more like a hollow-eyed scarecrow than my old friend, and if he had not spoken my name, I wouldn't have been certain it was him. When we hugged, he felt so fragile I was afraid he might break. Our other friends arrived, and the four of us sat in Charlie's living room, making small talk. I was trying hard to adjust to the wasted sight of him, when the Charlie I remembered had been so robust and energetic.

After a half hour or so we headed to a favorite restaurant, sliding easily into a leather booth. Less than two years ago I had eaten with him at this same restaurant and watched him pack away an enormous platter of ribs with gusto, but this time he paid little attention to the menu. Instead we all chatted away, placing our orders when the waitress came around and catching each other up on news of work and family. Charlie and I sat shoulder to shoulder, and he seemed completely relaxed. In spite of his troubling condition, there was no tension in the air. The four of us laughed almost nonstop until the waitress brought our drinks. Then, because I was sitting on the inside of the booth nearest the dispenser for condiments, Charlie turned to me mid-sentence, waved his hand, and said, "Gimme some sugar." Without thinking, I turned my face to his and planted a kiss on his warm cheek.

"Old Charlie" would have flinched or turned away. Or died in embarrassed mortification as Keith and Jana laughed. "New Charlie" didn't. He accepted the kiss with grace and laughed right along with us, never batting an eye. After dinner he seemed tired and said he wasn't up for the movie but he'd sure had a good time and wanted us to do it again soon. We took him home, and the four of us huddled in a group hug on the sidewalk. Then he went upstairs alone. I got in my car to begin the drive home, and I think may have even congratulated myself on how well things had gone and how I had managed to appear as if Charlie's awful state hadn't upset me at all. I was still feeling quite good about my performance when I began to weep so hard I could not see and was forced to pull my car over to the side of the road to collect myself. I was afraid the visit had been our last. I didn't see how he could possibly live much longer, and seeing him so frail and weak broke my heart, no matter how well I'd hidden it.

A few days later my phone rang and Charlie's voice greeted me. "Hey," he said, "it sure was good to be with you guys the other night."

"It was good to be with you too," I said. "Let's don't wait so long to do it again."

Then he paused. "Leigh," he said, "I need to tell you something."

I thought I knew what was coming. I thought he was going to apologize for how bad he had looked, to say he hoped I hadn't been frightened by his appearance, or that he wished I had not seen him that way. But he surprised me. What he said instead was this: "I want you to know that I'm getting better. I hope you could see that, underneath it all, I'm getting better every day." He was dying, and we both knew it. But he was being healed too. He seemed freer, and easier, and more relaxed than I'd seen him in years. More comfortable in his own skin than he'd ever been. And at peace with the future in a way that was unimaginable to me. He *was* getting better . . . I *could* see it, and I told him so. He sounded exhausted, but there was a new ring of joy in his voice—of victory, almost.

"Love you," he said as we drew the conversation to a close. I couldn't remember him saying those words before, ever.

"Love you too," I said and hung up the phone. It would be the last time we spoke before his healing was complete. I believe the next time I see him, it will be the strong, healthy Charlie I remember, only better. And next time I'll be better too.

"For momentary, light affliction," wrote the apostle Paul (and he, of all people, should have known), "is producing for us an eternal weight of glory far beyond all comparison. . . . For the things which are seen are temporal, but the things which are not seen are eternal" (2 Cor. 4:17–18). We struggle with healing here and now, because we want to be healed *here and now*. God, however, is not constrained as we are by time. It means far less to him than it does to us. We would define healing as "recovery in order to avoid death." But God has already defeated death. To him it registers as little more than a blip on the endless radar screen of eternity.

When this life serves up sickness or ruin or decay, we hunker down in the safest places we know, prepare for the worst, and pray for the best. We get our game faces on and resolve to ride out the chaos, hoping to prevail. When we do survive, when we do manage to evade the reaper, when God does heal our sickness before he calls us home, we breathe life in more deeply and thank the One who granted us more of it. But I suspect we know well what we seldom say: that at its very best, this realm of ours is little more than a field hospital for broken soldiers. We're revived here, and many of us do get better. We're bandaged, mended, and strengthened to fight again another day. But that doesn't change the fact that others don't make it and that we ourselves will one day succumb.

Good people get sick and die, even on bright blue days. Things get broken, even in the midst of beauty. "We live on holy ground," writes Eugene Peterson. "We inhabit sacred space. This holy ground is subject to incredible violations. This sacred space suffers constant sacrilege. But no matter. The holiness is there. The sacredness is there."[4] Not only do things get broken in the midst of beauty, there is a special beauty in the midst of that brokenness. There is a weighty, honest glory in suffering well . . . and still more in dying fragrantly. And whether our brokenness is healed here in the now or in the distant "not yet," healing always comes, when it comes, at the hands of our wounded King.

Director Peter Jackson left my favorite chapter out of his wonderful movie adaptation of Tolkien's Return of the King. *The battle of the fields of Pelennor is passed, and "no few had fallen, renowned or nameless, captain or soldier; for it was a great battle and the full count of it no tale has told."[5] Aragorn the future king has survived and has come to the Houses of Healing, where Faramir, Eowyn, and Merry lie fallen. An old woman weeping at the bed of Faramir cries, "Would that there were kings in Gondor, as there were once upon a time, they say! For it is said in old lore: The hands of the king are the hands of a healer."[6] The great wizard Gandalf agrees, saying, "It is only in the coming of Aragorn that any hope remains for the sick that lie in the House."[7]*

Then Aragorn arrives and heals Faramir, and the lady-warrior Eowyn, and the brave hobbit Merry by crushing rare herbs and breathing upon them: "A keen wind blew through the window, and it bore no scent, but was an air wholly fresh and clean and young, as if it had not before been breathed by any living thing and came new-made from snowy mountains high beneath a dome of stars, or from shores of silver far away washed by seas of foam."[8]

The hands of the King have healed me too. From sickness and from sorrow, from broken hearts and broken bones, from sin and from sadness, and from grief that seemed too great to bear. I have never placed myself in those hands and regretted the choice to do so, even when the result was not what I might have hoped. When and how have you been healed? For what healing do you still wait? Can you see the beauty of your brokenness or another's—and believe in the weight of glory that will one day be yours?

"For I consider that the sufferings of this present time are not worth comparing with the glory that is to be revealed to us. For the creation waits with eager longing for the revealing of the sons of God. For the creation was subjected to futility, not willingly, but because of him who subjected it, in hope that the creation itself will be set free from its bondage to decay and obtain the freedom of the glory of the children of God" (Rom. 8:18–21 ESV).

"Surely he has borne our griefs and carried our sorrows; yet we esteemed him stricken, smitten by God, and afflicted. But he was wounded for our transgressions; he was crushed for our iniquities; upon him was the chastisement that brought us peace, and with his stripes we are healed" (Isa. 53:4–5 ESV).

"So we do not lose heart. Though our outer nature is wasting away, our inner nature is being renewed day by day. For this slight, momentary affliction is preparing for us an eternal weight of glory beyond all comparison" (2 Cor. 4:16–17 ESV).

Scrabble in Stocking Feet

The Ache of Expecting

The house lights go off and the footlights come on. Even the chattiest stop chattering as they wait in darkness for the curtain to rise. In the orchestra pit, the violin bows are poised. The conductor has raised his baton.

Frederick Buechner

There's hardly a better going-to-sleep than the going-to-sleep of Christmas Eve. The expectation of the morning just a few hours away is shot through with so much wonder and delight that just keeping still and quiet is a challenge. We are made to anticipate . . . and we'll surely have more practice at it than we will at having whatever it is we wait for. But if we refuse to give ourselves over to the fullness of expectation, we lose twice: We miss the richness in the longing and the joy that comes when the sun rises on the day we've hungered for.

I love so many things about Christmas. There's Leroy Anderson's playfully orchestrated "Sleigh Ride." Or the Salvation Army bell ringers with their shiny red pots who wish hurried shoppers well, whether they offer their spare change or not. I adore the fragrance of freshly cut trees, the giddy rush of finding the perfect gift, and the sheer joy of receiving mail—lots of it—with real handwriting on each envelope.

Every December I'm sure to watch *It's a Wonderful Life*, though I know much of its dialogue by heart. And it's always good to hear gentle Linus recite the familiar verses from Luke's Gospel to the Charlie Brown gang, or Boris Karloff report that "the Grinch's small heart grew three sizes that day." Mass media aside, I can always entertain myself, making my own private survey of Christmases past, unwrapping and cherishing each memory as if it were a favorite, fragile ornament.

I recall a Christmas with my mother's family in West Texas when the neighbor's lonely German shepherd slipped in an open door and joined us in the living room, clambering up on the couch and taking one uncle's spot nearest the tree. (The dog looked friendly enough, but no one tried to move him, just in case.)

And another holiday with my dad's family when my Baptist deacon grandfather, overwhelmed with the joy of having all of us together under one roof, had a little too much eggnog and, buttoning the top button of his shirt collar, insisted he'd like to take my mother out dancing.

I've had Christmases pregnant with surprise, others that held few, and even one that brought improbable snow. But the sweetest yet was the one that *didn't* deliver the hoped-for gift . . . that didn't completely satisfy the longing it inspired.

The Christmas I'd call best so far was the one I almost spent with a man I loved twice—one I double-mindedly prayed would either lead to something lasting or at least not add the kind of new memories I'd have to work hard to forget. I wanted it to be wonderful or horrible—all good or all bad—and it was neither. God must have seen past my shortsighted, bet-hedging request, because my holiday that year was crammed full of mostly good moments, lots of them, strung together like tiny lights, each one a glowing reminder that once upon a cold December, we were at home with one another.

That Christmas we made snow angels, shopped in three states and veered into Canada, sang, and played Scrabble in our stocking feet. Our comfort barely lasted into January, but I still treasure it, even now.

I knew by May of that year that I loved him, and I didn't plan to. He snuck in the back door—the one I'd left open just in case but never expected someone to be resourceful enough to find or brave enough to use. I can't pinpoint an exact moment that I fell, but I was becoming more and more aware he made my days better just by being there. Two thirtysomething people who have never married can collect more than a few odd habits, and it would be fair to say we had both accumulated our share. When he announced in mid-July that we needed to take a break, I was hurt but not surprised. He said he didn't know where "it" was going; he wasn't sure if I was the one. I wasn't sure of him either, but I knew this: I liked our "it" a lot better than anything that had come before.

By October we were talking again, and by November he'd managed to edge his way back into my heart, even against my better judgment. I was working on a writing deadline, down to the wire by December and spending long days alone at the computer, pressing hard to finish. I'd become intimately acquainted with the 1:00 a.m. to 3:00 a.m. television time slot, leaving the box on for company as I clicked away at the keyboard. Martha Stewart's voice meant 2:00 a.m., and her crisply enunciated, matter-of-fact tone was annoying enough to set my teeth on edge. Martha would never have let *her* project get this far behind.

I was struggling then, and he rescued me. It was as simple as that. He called two or three times a day to ask what page I was on, and instead of being annoyed, I was encouraged. Once I told him I desperately needed "thirty minutes of fun," and in less than that time he was at my door with keys in hand. The "fun" he invented on the fly involved three dozen eggs and a four-story parking garage. I'd best leave it at that. But for those thirty minutes I laughed—hard—and it felt just right.

A few nights before I finished the book, with just a handful of pages to go and the end finally in sight, he called and asked if he could share with his mother the poem I had written my family and friends for Christmas. I said sure, of course he could.

"Or you could give it to her yourself," he said.

"Will I be seeing your mother anytime soon?"

"You will if you come home with me for Christmas."

His invitation caught me completely off guard. What in the world did it mean? We weren't dating anymore. Why should I trust him again? How foolish would it be to go off with the man who'd broken my heart without at least having a sober conversation as to where we might be headed?

By morning I still didn't know what was right, but I knew this: I wanted the feeling of leaving with him more than the feeling of being left behind. When he called we made this deal: I would go home with him for a few days before Christmas, but I needed to be back in Houston with my family by Christmas Eve. He agreed

143

and it was arranged. We would drive to Pennsylvania together, and he would put me on a southbound plane from Cleveland on December 24. I finished the manuscript, threw some warm clothes in a suitcase, and we left on a Saturday night, planning to drive until we got there—a twenty-two-hour experiment in proximity, uncertainty, and courage.

We traveled light. Between us we had one suitcase, a duffle bag, a couple of pillows, and a massive stack of CDs—but that was just the baggage you could see. Billy Joel, The Beatles, Sinatra, and show tunes provided road music, and he made a game of trying to guess my favorite song on every disc we played. He didn't miss many. He drove through the night, and I took the wheel as the sun came up in Memphis. It seemed odd to watch him sleeping, especially in daylight. "Wake me up when we get to West Virginia," he said, and in no more than a minute, he was out.

How full can a heart be? How much of the precious presence of another can it take in without breaking apart and spilling over onto everything? During those five days, I think I came close to knowing. The series of events is mostly jumbled now, and I'm sure I couldn't report in accurate fashion even a single day's itinerary. But I remember moments. And then one remembered moment invites the next one, and another after that, until a shimmering garland of delight and desire surrounds me.

When I opened my door that first morning at his parents' house, I found a newspaper folded on the floor—one that he'd gotten sometime after I fell asleep, because from Kentucky to Pennsylvania I had looked for a Sunday paper and not found one. And I remember lying on the floor poring over a scrapbook of old photographs of his parents when they were younger than we were, and at him in the mostly awkward years that I missed. I took a bath each morning in the same pink-tiled tub he'd soaked in as a kid, and I sat in my robe with his mom and dad at the breakfast table, cupping a steaming coffee mug in both hands.

We bargain shopped at an outdoor market called Pechin's and scratched off a single state lottery ticket but didn't win. We visited his sister in the bookstore where she worked and bought a book of Christmas poems there. When we left she gave me a brightly wrapped little box that held a small figurine—an unexpected gift from someone I'd never before met.

One night we played Scrabble with some neighbor friends down the street, our shoes kicked off under their table and our wits locked in determined battle above it. He would win, but he eased my hurt at being bested by covering my cold feet with his and rubbing them warm as he played out his tiles.

We drove to a resort in the Pennsylvania woods and walked its grounds and almost-empty rooms until nearly dusk. And then we drove some more. We had lunch in Pittsburgh one day with a friend of his from high school, and when we left the restaurant the clouds were heavy with snow and the air so cold it stung my face.

The last night we were with his parents, we watched a rented movie, *Zorro*, and then they went up to bed. I followed not far behind, but after I'd snuggled down beneath an extra blanket and turned out the light, he tapped softly on my door and invited me back downstairs. Curled up together in the dark, he asked if I wondered why he'd brought me there and if I was glad I'd come. "I'm just happy to be where you are," I whispered into his collarbone, and I was. But even those few words spoken out loud made me fearful that the safe, easy bubble we were floating in would burst.

That was it, really. There was no special gift that Christmas—actually no gift at all—and no words that might answer my nagging questions or calm my anxiety about where we might go from

145

there. Just his sweet presence, from morning into night, for five days straight. It was better than good. It was very nearly joy.

For five days I was Cinderella in a big ball gown, with music and motion and the pleasure of again being with someone who'd seemed lost to me forever. But it was edging closer to midnight, and I knew it. The last night we drove from Niagara Falls to Toronto for dinner, then back around Lake Erie to Cleveland in the wee hours of the morning. It was pitch dark and snowing, and it seemed like we were the only two people awake in the world. We talked about the summer before and what had happened since.

He told me he'd dated some, but that he'd compared every other girl to me. "She's cute," he said, "but she's not Leigh." Or, "She's bright, but not as bright as Leigh." Or funny. Or sweet. Or kind. Then he said something like this: "It's like taking a glass and filling it—first with stones, and you pile them to the top, but there are empty spaces. Then you try pebbles, and the fit is better, but still there are pockets where nothing goes. But if you take water, and pour it in, you fill it completely—no empty spaces at all. You're like that. You fit me. You're like water over stones."

I don't remember saying anything. I couldn't. I was too close to tears. It was the eleventh hour in the middle of nowhere, and one of us had finally told the truth. Not long after that we switched places and I began to drive. He fell asleep and I cried hard—hot tears that ran down my face and neck and dropped into my lap one after another. But I didn't make a sound. I knew if I woke him I'd have to explain, and I couldn't pull the words up from my heart into my mouth. He'd been with me for five days, fully present but just slightly out of reach. In a few short hours I would have to say goodbye again on the curb of another airport. And what then? What then? I wanted more of him, and I didn't believe I would have it. The ball was over. The music had stopped. And I was going home alone.

146

Maybe it's the expectation of Christmas that is best. The longing. The waiting. Hope deferred, but with the anticipation of sure pleasure just ahead. The event itself might be something of a blur, but the days leading up to it—those are achingly ripe and sweet.

Before Jesus entered recorded history in Bethlehem of Judea, a Messiah was the hope of every devout Jew. They were waiting. *"O come, O come, Emmanuel, and ransom captive Israel, that mourns in lonely exile here until the Son of God appear."* What a mystery that man would wait for what had always existed! Wait for what never *wasn't*, according the apostle John: "In the beginning was the Word, and the Word was with God, and the Word was God. He was with God in the beginning. Through him all things were made; without him nothing was made that has been made" (John 1:1–3 NIV).

In the beginning he was with God, but in the fullness of time, he became God *with us*. Emmanuel. At Christmas his eternal presence became tangible, seeable. He had skin and hair and a tiny soft spot in his newly formed skull. He cried real tears and tried out his human voice the way we all do: thrust from a warm, safe womb and gasping hard for air.

He was nothing like us, and he was one of us. His true home was heaven, and even so, he willingly stooped to enter human hearts. His presence was so real, so true, that years later John, as an old man nearing death, would recall, "That which was from the beginning, which we have heard, which we have seen with our eyes, which we have looked at and our hands have touched—this we proclaim concerning the Word of life. The life appeared; we have seen it and testify to it, and we proclaim to you the eternal life, which was with the Father and has appeared to us" (1 John 1:1–2 NIV).

Presence. God with us. Emmanuel. John didn't rehash miracles as he neared the end of his days on earth—and he had been privy to them all. He'd seen water turned to wine. Bread multiplied. Blindness healed. Seas stilled. The resurrected Christ cooking breakfast on the shore in Galilee. No, he simply remembered Christ's everyday presence. "I saw him," John said, "and I am still seeing him. I touched him with my own hands. I heard his voice, and I am hearing it still." He remembered the power of the daily, common, ordinary presence of One whom he loved and One who loved him.

Once, in college, I dated a man who was master of the grand gesture. He put his money where it showed and majored in the big moments. But sometimes he was mean. And in between the big moments were unkind comments and small lapses in common courtesy. An older woman I knew, who was married with three daughters, talked to me one day about his inconsistency.

"He's good with the flowers," she noted. He was.

"Takes you out on Saturday night to nice places, doesn't he?" He did.

"But I've seen him say hurtful things to you," she added. And he had.

Then she said this: "You want to marry someone you can enjoy on a Tuesday night, because marriage is like a lot of Tuesday nights, all run together. Marry someone whose company you'll want to keep no matter what day it is."

I haven't forgotten that. But I'm sure I didn't entirely understand it until very lately. I thought at first she meant, "Dating may be fun, but long-term commitment is a rather dull and tedious program. Wait for a plodder who will finish the race, even if he doesn't run it in a very exciting way." I had missed by a mile.

The counsel she was gently offering was this: It is no small gift to find another who is like you and whose presence is so comforting and right that even the most ordinary moments are enriched by it. Better still is when that one whose presence is life-giving to you comes and means to stay. Emmanuel. God like us. God with us. Forever.

From the hotel in Cleveland to the airport nearby, I was mostly silent, lost in my own tumble of thoughts. I wished for a paper or something to read to keep me from having to make small talk after what had not been, for me at least, a small time. When we pulled up I got out, took my bag from his hands, and pressed into them a note that was meant to explain all that I felt but couldn't speak. I didn't want to say goodbye again. I didn't want to wonder if the tenderness of the last few days would ever repeat itself. And then, after a quick embrace, I turned and walked into the terminal without looking back. I was smarter than Lot's wife. I knew my limitations.

A crowd of people was already jostling at the gate. It was Christmas Eve, and they were going home—the best of their holiday still in front of them, waiting to unfold. They were buzzing with energy and anticipation. But my Christmas was already behind me. I had been full, but now I was empty. I'd tasted goodness, but I wasn't nearly satisfied. They were moving toward what they longed for; I was moving away. For a full ten minutes I trained my eyes on the corridor I'd just walked through, hoping against hope that he might have read my words and decided to come back. I stood straining to glimpse someone in the distance with his gait, the set of his shoulders, his height, and his frame.

As the call came to begin boarding the flight, I nudged my bag forward with my feet and glanced down the corridor one more time. If my life were a movie, he would have appeared around a corner, spotted my searching face, and hurried toward me just in time. Then the credits would begin to roll. Movie credits are a useful device, because you can believe whatever you most wanted to happen *is* happening somewhere while the names of the caterer, the gaffer, and the best boy are drifting down the screen.

But he didn't come. I stowed my bag in the overhead compartment, took my seat, pulled my seat belt snug, and closed my eyes. When I did I saw the lights on Niagara Falls at night, heard Van Morrison's "Moondance" in a Toronto café, and felt his breath on my face as he wrapped my scarf around my head and tucked the edges in my coat the way he did each time we stepped out of the car and into the cold . . . and I fell asleep remembering the uncomplicated goodness of his presence.

Why would a holiday full of simple nearness and a yearning for more of it make my list of favorites? Why not one where the right gift arrived just in time or the whole family made it home?

Because this is the now and the not yet. Because here we taste only a little of the treasure that is ours. Because it's the very longing that makes the eventual receiving truly sweet. Had those who loved Jesus best not suffered the crushing blow of his death, how could they have savored the massive joy of resurrection morning? The answer is simple: They couldn't have.

All that had come before prepared them for what would come after and for what is still yet to come. The incarnation opened a one-way door to the crucifixion. The crucifixion was a minor-key prelude to the resurrection. And the resurrection brought with it another kind of presence—the promised presence of the Spirit, who sustains us with the indwelling nearness of the bridegroom until he comes again to claim us as his. Christ has come. Christ is here. Christ will come again. Emmanuel. God with us.

This to me *is* Christmas: a lovely and joyful beginning to a story still unfolding. Yes, it uncovers longings it never quite satisfies, but only because it wasn't meant to. That's another chapter, saved for another time. At its best, the Advent season carries the expectation of a presence that will never be broken by goodbyes—births a love that is almost too good to believe. And it would be a fairy story of the cruelest kind except for this: It's entirely true. I know, because I've been to the ball with the Prince of Peace—and in his perfect presence, nothing changed at midnight.

Have you ever wanted something so much you were afraid to admit it? Afraid that saying it out loud might mean never having it at all—or fearful of looking foolish if the longed-for thing never arrives? Editing down desire is a tricky business. There is a fine line between sublimating expectation and denying it. And it's so very hard to tell when you've crossed from one to the other.

How good is it to have a God who's made promises—wild ones!—and kept them? Who is keeping them still? How sweet to fall asleep to the lullaby of longing that he sings and wake up every morning searching for brand-new evidence of his arrival. And what a shame to deny that we're dying to do just that—not once a year but over and over until time cannot be counted anymore.

"I will betroth you to Me forever; yes, I will betroth you to Me in righteousness and in justice, in lovingkindness and in compassion, and I will betroth you to Me in faithfulness. Then you will know the LORD" (Hosea 2:19–20).

151

"But as for you, Bethlehem Ephrathah, too little to be among the clans of Judah, from you One will go forth for Me to be ruler in Israel. His goings forth are from long ago, from the days of eternity. . . . And He will arise and shepherd His flock in the strength of the LORD, in the majesty of the name of the LORD His God. And they will remain, because at that time He will be great to the ends of the earth. This One will be our peace" (Micah 5:2, 4–5).

New Clothes for Cara

The Ache for Beauty

> Tale as old as time,
> Song as old as rhyme,
> Beauty and the Beast.
>
> Howard Ashman and Tim Rice,
> "Beauty and the Beast"

We gravitate toward beauty, longing both to be beautiful and to surround ourselves with beautiful things. Beauty points us God-ward in ways we can't explain. The Sistine Chapel calls forth a yearning for the Eternal Source of beauty, just as surely as a field of wildflowers or a blanket of fresh snow can evoke his praise. We humans thirst for beauty and ache at the gulf between the faint hints of it we experience here and the dazzling reality that waits somewhere past the edges of this world.

A single scene from Disney's *Beauty and the Beast* causes a lump to form in my throat every time I see it. Maybe you've seen it too. The tough-but-tender heroine Belle is waltzing through an empty ballroom with the ugly, hulking Beast, and she's smiling up at his hideous face, her ingénue eyes aglow. It's one of those strange moments where love creeps in against all odds and insists on staying put; where beauty is fixed utterly and completely in the eye of the beholder and is not about to budge.

I took my nieces to see this film when they were younger, very likely as "cover" (I had wanted to see it myself but felt a bit too old to go without underage accomplices). Afterward, driving home in the car, I asked them both what part of the story they liked best. My youngest niece, Victoria, seven or eight at the time, piped up breathlessly from the back seat: "Oh, Aunt Leigh—I loved it when she danced with him . . . and he was still the Beast." (So did I!) In that cavernous ballroom, love made something hideous quite lovely. And even a child could see it.

Although I've hunted beauty like big game almost all my life, I've rarely felt truly and unquestionably beautiful. I suspect few women really do. Maybe that's why cosmetics companies are mostly recession-proof and why ordinary-looking people buy fashion magazines containing nothing an ordinary-looking person would ever wear. Even as we faithfully collect and perfect the tricks of *appearing* beautiful, deep down most of us still feel decidedly "less than." Less than lovely. Less than photogenic. Less than artfully original. Less than the man or woman next to us, who probably feels "less than" too.

Why? Why in our hearts do we cast ourselves as Cinderella *before* some fairy godmother does her wand-waving makeover? Why do we wish for another's hair or hips or lips or eyes? Why, even on our best days, do we detect a needling whisper that says "not good enough" or "nice try, but . . ."? And why will a woman whose beauty is openly praised by another immediately point out her secret flaw, as if a disclaimer is somehow required for truth's sake?

Because we're not sure. *I'm* not sure. I'm not sure I can trust my own eyes, or a great hall of mirrors, or the woman in the next dressing room, or my best friend. And even if I could, I'd still know what they all don't, and can't: I'm flawed on the inside, even when I'm outwardly displaying my best. I long to be beautiful—but I can't put much stock in my own well-nurtured attractiveness. I know far too well what imperfections I'm hiding.

Part of the wonder of childhood is that you get to keep your compliments. Children are naturally, unabashedly self-centered and prone to matter-of-factly trust the good things others say about them. It's not considered conceit when you're five or six to believe that your eyes are pretty or your freckles adorable. Not yet. The delight of early praise is that it need not be deflected or dodged or denied. Children can actually *bask* in it if they want and appear just as pleased as they really are to be momentarily admired, even by a stranger.

It's no wonder that children loved the lap of Jesus and clamored to be close to him. As he called their names and touched their heads and winked at them, he must have offered the sort of easy praise that makes young hearts fairly somersault with joy:

"Ah, Leah, what a wonderful laugh you have! Let me hear it again, will you?"

"Thomas! Show me those muscles in your arms—look how strong you are!"

"Anna, my sweet, your eyes sparkle like jewels! They're wonderful!"

God-in-the-flesh would have seen and celebrated each little one's unique glories and perfectly reflected them back. And they would have undoubtedly believed him.

It's also no wonder that the disciples grumbled at this. They were too big for the lap they wished they might rest in and too ashamed to admit they longed for his affirming words just as much or more than the little ones they self-righteously shooed away.

We understand those disciples because we're like them: We're big people with little people's yearning hearts. We long to be told we're lovely by the One whose opinion is beyond dispute. We long to be in the presence of loveliness. And we ache to shed the shame that seems to accumulate in adulthood in favor of a child's winsome openness: to believe that we have absolutely nothing to hide and no good reason to do so.

Cara was a temporary ward of the state, and I was introduced to her through a court-appointed advocacy program. It was my job to champion her cause, working with parents, foster care providers, social workers, teachers, counselors, and the family courts to ensure that her short-term needs were met and that her future was as safe and secure as possible. For as long as it took to resolve her tumultuous living situation, I would be on Cara's side.

One hot Saturday morning in August, I and scores of other volunteers met our young charges in a chain store parking lot and prepared to back-to-school shop for them with donated gift certificates. We had the run of the store until it officially opened at 10:00 a.m. and the fun challenge of spending $100—tax free!—within our allotted amount of time.

Cara fidgeted in my lap as we waited to begin shopping. I'm not sure she understood that we were there for her—or that we were about to buy more new clothes than she had likely ever gotten at once. When the sponsors gave the word, we were quickly off, weaving our way through the crowded racks, searching for things in her size and holding them up for closer inspection.

She liked purple, she told me, and pink. My earlier experiences with Cara had confirmed that she was both a girly-girl *and* a tomboy—a delightful combination of daintiness and daring—so we needed both dresses and shorts, ruffles and T-shirts, and, she suggested shyly, "maybe something with sparkles." I added the price tags up in my head as we went, we gathered an armful of possibilities and veered toward the dressing rooms, where the real fun would begin.

Because there were over one hundred children and volunteers in the store at once, the line to try things on was long. Many girls were changing in the corridors outside the dressing rooms, but Cara shook her little head "no" when I asked if she wanted to do the same. So we waited for a fitting room of our own. When one opened up, I carried her things in and hung them one by one. While she removed her shirt and shorts, I unzipped the first outfit and held it out to her. She slipped the dress over her head, and I zipped her up, tugging down the hem and smoothing out the shoulders.

Cara turned and faced the mirror, barely smiling and with her eyes down. "Do you like it?" I asked. She silently nodded yes. Then she opened the dressing room door and stepped into the hallway.

Another volunteer who saw her immediately praised her outfit: "Oh, honey—that looks so pretty on you!" Cara giggled and dashed back inside. We hung that dress up and proceeded to the next one. After looking at herself in the mirror again, she twirled a little—a tiny pirouette that made my heart glad. She clearly

New Clothes for Cara

liked what she saw reflected in the glass. Then she opened the dressing room door again and twirled for her "outside" audience. The response was overwhelmingly positive.

For several minutes we repeated this routine. Cara dressed, twirled before the mirror, took her turn on the hallway "catwalk" to cries of delight, and returned to me to help her into the next outfit. After her fourth or fifth turn, she came back in, threw herself across my lap, twisted sideways to look up at me, and said in a confessional whisper, "I'm showing off." I felt my throat tighten and my eyes mist over.

"I know, sweetie, and that's okay," I whispered back. If I could have bought the whole store for her, I would have. An hour and a hasty Happy Meal later, our bags were stuffed with clothes, socks, underwear, and tennis shoes. The store had generously donated a backpack and school supplies for each child. It was Christmas in August. Cara had seen in the mirror a beautifully dressed little girl she'd never seen before, and, even better, she'd seen her own beauty reflected in the eyes of others. It may have been the first time, but I hoped it would happen many times over in the days and years to come. She needed to feel beautiful. And she *was* beautiful. But it took someone else to help her believe and enjoy it.

The Gospel of John records another story of ugliness redeemed and beauty revealed. We don't know the woman's name, but her circumstance could not have been more shameful or humiliating. She was caught in an adulterous liaison, and her accusers were bent on using her ugly secret to challenge the new rabbi in town. "They made her stand before the group and said to Jesus, 'Teacher, this woman was caught in the act of adultery. In the law Moses commanded us to stone such women. Now what do you say?' They were using this question as a trap, in order to have a basis for accusing him" (John 8:3–6 NIV).

Can't you see it? She's cowering naked, or nearly so. She is surrounded by contentious, angry men—and she's the only one exposed. Not just her flesh, either. Her private sin has just become public. Her secret is out. The men shouting around her can hide the ugliness of their own mistakes, but hers is out in the open for all to see.

To me, mercy in this situation would have called for immediate resolution. If I had been this woman, I would have wanted Jesus, the good rabbi, to hush them and to cover me. I would have wanted the episode to be over quickly. For him to send them away and then to leave himself so that I could slink off in shame and remorse—or for him to condemn me quickly and let me die. It didn't happen that way. In what must have seemed an excruciatingly painful delay, the Son of God did this instead: "But Jesus bent down and started to write on the ground with his finger" (John 8:6 NIV). Finger painting in the dust! Couldn't he instead scatter them in righteous anger the way he dispersed the money changers in the temple? Or at least throw his cloak over her and let her hide her face, if not her body?

"When they kept on questioning him, he straightened up and said to them, 'If any one of you is without sin, let him be the first to throw a stone at her.' Again he stooped down and wrote on the ground" (John 8:7–8 NIV).

What was this? He had turned the focus from her sin to theirs! It had never occurred to her that such a thing could happen. She hadn't thought for a moment about *their* sin, only her own. Now he was asking them to stop examining her (and testing him) and to search their own hearts instead. And as they did, she heard the unmistakable sound of rocks—the rocks they had threatened to kill her with—dropping with heavy thuds in the dust. She heard their murmuring turn to silence and their feet shuffling away. And then she was alone. Only one man was left. And he had not accused her.

"Jesus straightened up and asked her, 'Woman, where are they? Has no one condemned you?' 'No one, sir,' she said. 'Then neither do I condemn you,' Jesus declared. 'Go now and leave your life of sin'" (John 8:10–11 NIV).

He was standing next to her now, looking into her eyes and telling her that he would not condemn her. Not that she wasn't guilty—but that her guilt wasn't final or fatal. By leaving this woman exposed for those few agonizing moments, he had uncovered her accusers' sins too. They had made her feel like the only sinner in the world. He let her know she was not. He didn't say, "I'm sure they were mistaken about you." He knew they were telling the truth. He saw who she was *and* what she had done. But he also saw more. He saw a woman whose heart yearned to be loved and to be lovely. So he commanded her to do something she had never before considered a possibility—especially in light of *this* day's events. He told her to leave her old life behind and begin again.

In his eyes she saw forgiveness and mercy. In his kindness she met repentance. And in his beautiful, holy presence, something of her became beautiful too.

We hunger for beauty because we know what this accused woman knew: We have secrets, and we have fallen far from grace. We long for beauty because we have flaws to hide, and yet in some intangible way, we're drawn like moths to the revealing light of truth and goodness. Any finery we can conjure for ourselves from the world's resources is a cheap substitute for *his* sinless beauty—and our shabby attempts at goodness are no match for his blazing righteousness. We ache for our lovely, unfallen state; we pine for the pristine perfection of Eden. We don't get them here—but we long for them just the same.

That's why we cover ourselves with the best "robes" money can buy and surround ourselves with the most elaborate imitations of paradise that we can artfully arrange. But it's never enough, and we know it. True beauty isn't manufactured. It's reflected. And his perfect heart is the mirror that shows us how lovely we were meant to be and will, by his grace, one day become. Every glimpse of true beauty—his beauty—that comes in the meantime will whisper his name. "Beauty," said Pope John Paul II, "is a key to the mystery and a call to transcendence. It is an invitation to savor life and to dream of the future. That is why the beauty of created things can never fully satisfy. It stirs that hidden nostalgia for God."[1]

One day, the One who has made everything beautiful in its time will return to this fallen planet and call forth a new heaven and a new earth. So our longing for perfection will not be in vain. One day we will be utterly beautiful and surrounded by nothing *but* beauty. But until then, the ache will invade and inhabit every faint glimmer of loveliness that peeps through the veil. Until then, in the words of poet Gerard Manley Hopkins, our best examples of beauty will be fleeting and incomplete:

> Glory be to God for dappled things—
> > For skies of couple-colour as a brinded cow;
>
> . . . .
>
> All things counter original, spare, strange;
> > Whatever is fickle, freckled (who knows how?)
> > With swift, slow; sweet, sour; adazzle, dim;
> He fathers-forth whose beauty is past change:
> > Praise him.[2]

In the Disney version of that famous fairy tale, the Beast not only found beautiful Belle but *she* found the hidden beauty in *him*. She saw past his ugliness and shame to what he might become and loved him well beyond what seemed right or reasonable at the time. Thus loved, the Beast *became* beautiful too. My sweet friend Cara was surrounded by the ugliness of abuse and abandonment, but some new clothes and a stranger's encouragement coaxed her own beauty into fragile bloom. Love is like that. It calls forth what it alone sees—and transforms for good what it touches.

Which one of us doesn't want to be loved when we're hopelessly unlovely? Who doesn't hope for a hero who sees us at our very worst and steadfastly refuses to be repulsed? Beauty and the Beast really *is* a "tale as old as time," and the oldest, truest version of it goes something like this: "You see, at just the right time, when we were still powerless, Christ died for the ungodly. Very rarely will anyone die for a righteous man, though for a good man someone might possibly dare to die. But God demonstrates his own love for us in this: While we were still sinners, Christ died for us" (Rom. 5:6–8 NIV).

The Old Testament saints could not see God (and his awesome, undiluted beauty) face-to-face and hope to live. But in Jesus, man has seen, touched, and handled the Beautiful One and not only lived to tell but found in him the promise of eternal life and unending beauty. He *is* beauty. And he alone makes us beautiful. Nothing less will ever be enough.

The best moments of a wedding are those when the groom first sees his bride. Sure, he's seen her many, many times before—but never once like this: never so perfectly attired and beautifully arrayed; never as hopefully lovely or full of desire. Whatever the story of any bride and groom, it comes down to this: He has chosen her. And it is that chosenness, more than anything, that makes her beautiful. Her loveliness is demonstrated in a hundred details, but it began and resides in the eyes of her groom. We are Jesus's bride, and his aim is to make us beautiful. Until we gaze into his face and see our reflection there, we will not begin to believe he has already done so.

"They looked to Him and were radiant, and their faces will never be ashamed" (Ps. 34:5).

"Listen, O daughter, consider and give ear: Forget your people and your father's house. The king is enthralled by your beauty; honor him, for he is your lord" (Ps. 45:10–11 NIV).

"In that day the Branch of the LORD will be beautiful and glorious, and the fruit of the land will be the pride and glory of the survivors in Israel. Those who are left in Zion, who remain in Jerusalem, will be called holy, all who are recorded among the living in Jerusalem" (Isa. 4:2–3 NIV).

12

Old Addresses

The Ache of Memory

Let memory have its way. It is a minister of God with its rebuke and chastisement and sorrow. God will turn the "what might have been" into a wonderful culture for the future.

Oswald Chambers, *My Utmost for His Highest*

Each of us has a story. My story is much like yours and yet quite different from yours. It is a tragedy, a comedy, an epic adventure, a fairy tale, and a romance. It embraces every place I've ever lived and every person I've ever loved. It's messy and memorable, sweet and sad, mundane and miraculous. But more than anything, it's mine. Woven into every word and line, redeeming every hurtful chapter and making the richest parts even richer is the beautiful Storyteller who wooed and won my heart so near the beginning and has not, cannot, will not let it go.

*O*ur small family had already migrated nearly 3,800 miles from Honolulu, Hawaii, to a three-bedroom brick house at 807 Huisache Street in Refugio, Texas, by the time I was two—but the Huisache house is the first home I remember. A tree large enough to climb stood in the front yard, and a chain-link fence surrounded the back. I practiced tap dancing on the front porch so I wouldn't scuff the waxed and shiny floors inside, and I learned to ride my tricycle down the driveway and back. We lived on Huisache until I was six, and there my older sister and I shared a room—our two twin beds fixed like comfortable, floating islands with a throw rug of a river in between.

This was the house where I learned to read, looking over my sister's shoulder at her kindergarten books and softly sounding out the words. In this safe, small-town cocoon, routines reinforced the edges of family life. Dad went to work in the morning, and Mother stayed home with us. Breakfast, lunch, and dinner were served at the same time every day, and bedtime came at the same time each night. We went to church on Sunday, rain or shine, where we heard the same Bible stories and sang the same songs week after week.

Our little family of four seemed picture-perfect to me, and it must have looked it too. I felt safe—and I was—but through our foundation ran hidden fault lines that I could not see yet some-how sensed. I suspect that now because the game my sister and I most often played on Huisache was not a typical childhood game like hopscotch or hide-and-seek or tag. Our favorite game was a self-styled one we called "run away from our boyfriends," and I don't remember having any other friends who played it.

The plot of "run away from our boyfriends" was illogically simple: We took our plastic phone and called our boyfriends at the office, telling them we were leaving and taking the babies with us. If they wanted to find us, we said, they would have to come looking. We never divulged our planned destination, even though they always begged us for it. Once the phone call was made, we gathered our dolls and dressed them for the road, then packed two tiny, red pasteboard suitcases with more of their clothes and a few small toys and books. Our exodus never extended beyond our bedroom door, but we set up camp in "away from home" tents made from our bedcovers, using our batons as tent poles. And although I don't remember enacting this part, the boyfriends must have found us and we must have gone back home each time, because we ran away from them over and over again.

I honestly don't recall this scenario or anything like it ever being played out in real life, so I can't say what the genesis of our game might have been. But an invisible undercurrent existed in our warm, well-ordered little house on Huisache, a vague hint of upset or uncertainty that couldn't be seen with the naked eye. Our game reinforced the notion that even the surest refuge wasn't foolproof—and that flight was an ever-ready ace in the hole.

My earliest ancestors' first address was a rural one—a lush garden called Eden situated somewhere in the fertile valleys of the Tigris and Euphrates rivers. God placed Adam there and charged him with keeping and cultivating the spread. But as beautiful as it must have been, even Eden contained the potential to go awry: "The LORD God planted a garden toward the east, in Eden; and there He placed the man whom He had formed. Out of the ground the LORD God caused to grow every tree that is pleasing to the sight and good for food; the tree of life also in the midst of the garden, and the tree of the knowledge of good and evil" (Gen. 2:8–9).

As fine as this lovingly crafted paradise was, it wasn't impervious to the whims of man. To make sure Adam understood the inherent danger, God clearly instructed him: "From any tree of the garden you may eat freely; but from the tree of the knowledge of good and evil you shall not eat, for in the day that you eat from it you will surely die" (Gen. 2:16–17). Clear enough, but we know the next bit of the story well—especially since we've been reenacting it ever since. "Now the serpent was more crafty than any beast of the field which the LORD God had made. And he said to the woman, 'Indeed, has God said, "You shall not eat from any tree of the garden"?'" (Gen. 3:1).

Eve replied that there was only one tree among all the trees in the garden that she and Adam had been warned about—and that eating from *that* tree would cause them to die. Satan disputed her claim, offering her the very fruit God had forbidden. She ate. Adam ate. And innocence was gone forever. The beautiful, pristine paradise that had nurtured them now seemed threatening. They saw their nakedness and tried their best to cover it. They felt flawed and vulnerable. And they were. When God came calling, they ran from him and hid. And when he found them and questioned them, they confessed. He covered them with animal skins, since their nakedness was no longer comfortable to them, and sent Adam out from the Garden of Eden "to cultivate the ground from which he was taken. So He drove the man out; and at the east of the garden of Eden He stationed the cherubim and the flaming sword which turned every direction to guard the way to the tree of life" (Gen. 3:23–24).

Every memory of ours bears an undercurrent of sin because once upon a time, our ancestors let it in. And we've been running away ever since. Even though I was barely old enough to tie my

169

own sneakers, I knew on Huisache Street that something dark swam past the edges of my awareness . . . something I could not tame or forever keep at bay. But God was covering me even then, and he kept me from running far.

The house we lived in longest was a suburban ranch on the southwest side of the city, a brand-new house where we carved the year "1967" on the still-wet cement of the garage stoop. In our house on Triola Lane, almost everything felt new. My faith was new, and a passion for music and poetry bloomed at almost the same time. I wrote my first poem in longhand on the huge desk in the middle bedroom just days after my baptism, fumbled through my first kiss on the front porch, and sank the first of many free throws in the basketball hoop in the back. In that Triola house, I fell in love more than once, but the sweetest fall and longest crush stretched from my sophomore year in high school to my sophomore year in college.

I adored this boy and pined for him when we were apart. Even when I dated others, his was the call I waited for; his was the company I loved best. He tutored me in geometry and wrote endearing words to me in yearbooks and on napkins and the backs of photographs. We had no more than a handful of dates before he went away to college, but we remained in touch. Our families became friends, and I suspect even they thought we might wind up together. (My father must have; he let me know in no uncertain terms when I left for the same school two years later that if I married before I finished college, the remainder of my tuition tab would be my lucky husband's responsibility.)

Our friendship remained deep and constant, only occasionally veering into the romantic realm; he did just enough to keep my hopes alive but never so much as to make me certain of them. Still, I believed in us, and his presence became my security. That is, until the day I rode my bicycle to a small park to study and nearly stumbled over him lying on the grass, his arms and legs entwined with a girl I'd never seen before. I was so stunned I couldn't speak—I ran away before he could see me. On the way back to my dorm room, sobbing and shaking, I sliced my heel on the pedal of my bike and left a trail of bright red blood behind me. In the span of a few moments, my dearest hope was crucified. The person I depended on most had moved on without me knowing it, and he left behind an ache a mile wide and twice as deep.

The one I had long believed was my future apparently did not embrace the same assignment. But his painful demonstration of that fact made ample room for the One who *was* my future and would never leave. What I saw that day caused me to throw myself on Jesus in an awful, desperate way. There was simply nowhere else for me to go. My heart was hammered flat, but in time it reconstituted itself, stronger than before. I fell hard and bruised deeply, bruises that took years to disappear. If I said I knew then that the ache was for my good, I'd be lying. I didn't. But I do now.

Our memories possess the power to bless us or curse us. They may comfort or condemn, intruding helter-skelter with a mind of their own. "Suddenly," says writer Frederick Buechner, "there it all is—something that happened to us once—and it is there not just as a picture on the wall to stand back from and gaze at but as a reality we are so much a part of still and that is still so much a part of us, that we feel with something close to its original intensity and freshness . . . old failures, old hurts. Times too beautiful to tell or too terrible."[1]

The power of memory may frighten or bewitch us—so that we run from remembering, or else try to crawl back through time's tunnel and relive or revise those hours or days that no longer exist. "We cling to the present out of wariness of the past," says Buechner. "We cling to the surface out of fear of what lies beneath the surface."[2] But what if we did not have to be afraid? What if we met our memories, when they arrived, with the confidence of one who is held—not haunted—by Providence? What if we took the hand of Jesus and lingered long enough with each memory to be comforted, or taught, or forgiven, or released, grateful for where our stories have brought us, for what our past has made of us, for the ways that our memories connect us to one another and to the larger story God is still writing even now?

Only one disciple has traditionally taken the rap for deserting Jesus at the end, but really, at least two abandoned him. "I will strike the shepherd," wrote the prophet Zechariah, "and the sheep of the flock will be scattered" (Matt. 26:31 NIV). Judas and Peter hardly would have argued Zechariah's foretelling accuracy. The old address forever imprinted in Judas's memory was undoubtedly the Garden of Gethsemane, where he fingered the Son of God with a deliberate, deceitful kiss: "While [Jesus] was still speaking, Judas, one of the Twelve, arrived. With him was a large crowd armed with swords and clubs, sent from the chief priests and the elders of the people. Now the betrayer had arranged a signal with them: 'The one I kiss is the man; arrest him.' Going at once to Jesus, Judas said, 'Greetings, Rabbi!' and kissed him" (Matt. 26:47–49 NIV).

Whether Judas was disappointed in his teacher's lack of messianic ambition or hoping to force him into a confrontation with the Jewish authorities or simply tired of following, he intentionally aligned himself with Jesus's enemies and took their money to betray him. Judas himself even suggested the sign of a kiss—a special gesture of friendship and of respect—to identify the one he was abandoning.

"Friend," Jesus said to him, receiving the kiss, "do what you came for" (Matt. 26:50 NIV).

The next morning, as it became clear that Jesus's arrest would result in his death, Judas saw his teacher bound and led to the Roman governor's chamber, and he was overcome with deep remorse. "I have sinned," he told the chief priests and the elders, trying to return the money they had paid him, "for I have betrayed innocent blood" (Matt. 27:4 NIV). But they felt no sympathy for their partner in crime, refused to take back their thirty pieces of silver, and sent him on his way. Judas threw the blood money into the temple, Matthew's Gospel says, "then he went away and hanged himself" (27:5 NIV).

Judas's memory destroyed him. His contempt for what he had done fed an awful, self-loathing brand of sorrow that he believed only death could dismiss. The thought of living with the image of that kiss in the garden was too much. He couldn't bear another hour in the wake of what he had done.

But Peter too abandoned his teacher and friend. His betrayal came in the courtyard of the high priest, Caiaphas, while Jesus was being questioned inside. And he had even been warned that it was coming: "When they had sung a hymn, they went out to the Mount of Olives. Then Jesus told them, 'This very night you will all fall away on account of me'" (Matt. 26:30–31 NIV). Peter protested, "Even if all fall away on account of you, I never will" (v. 33 NIV). Jesus told him, "This very night, before the rooster crows, you will disown me three times" (v. 34 NIV).

It was unthinkable to Peter that Jesus's words could be true, but when caught off guard by a servant girl who said she had seen him with "Jesus of Galilee," he folded like a flimsy house of cards: "I don't know what you are talking about." He moved away from her, nearer the courtyard gate, where another young woman saw him and announced to those within earshot: "This fellow was with Jesus of Nazareth." He again denied it: "I don't know the man!" A little later someone else confronted him: "Surely you are one of them, for your accent gives you away." He was adamant in his denial, swearing again, "I don't know the man!" (Matt. 26:69–74 NIV).

Cruelly, as predicted, the crowing of a rooster reminded Peter of his cocky, self-assured claims and of Jesus's dead-on prediction. "And he went outside," Matthew's Gospel records, "and wept bitterly" (26:75 NIV).

There wasn't a night dark enough to cover what he'd done. There weren't enough tears to cleanse his conscience. He had failed his Lord, and himself. How ridiculously pathetic his claim of dying with Jesus must have sounded to his own ears! Unlike Judas, however, Peter remained nearby while his Savior was crucified, and he continued to live with his guilt rather than die under its weight. His conviction led him to sorrow, but a sorrow not unto death . . . but unto life.

Days after his death, Jesus appeared again to his disciples on the shore of the Sea of Galilee. Most of them had been fishermen; they simply went back to what they knew best. Only through this long night, they hadn't caught a single fish. From the shore he called out to them, "Friends, haven't you any fish?" (John 21:5 NIV). They told him no.

"Throw your net on the right side of the boat and you will find some," he told them, and when they followed his direction, their nets were filled with fish (v. 6 NIV). Whether it was the miraculous load of fish, or the sound of Jesus's voice, or just a hunch, John said to Peter, "It is the Lord!" and Peter jumped overboard to swim to him (v. 7 NIV).

Then a loving exchange on the shoreline gently replaced Peter's memory of his courtyard denial. "Simon son of John," Jesus said to him, "do you love me?" (v. 17 NIV). Three times Jesus asked him, and three times Peter professed his love. Each time Jesus ordered him, "Feed my sheep." The faithful shepherd was asking the failed fisherman to become a shepherd too and charging him with the care of the shepherd's own flock. Love took away Peter's shame and healed the memory of his emphatic denial. "God," said Oswald Chambers, "is prepared to run the risk of evil so to speak, and the cross is the proof that He Himself has taken the responsibility of its removal."[3]

Judas took his awful memory to heart and silenced it the only way *he* could silence it: by killing himself. Peter took his ache to the very One he'd wounded and in his presence saw it transformed and his hope renewed.

Whatever the old addresses of my memory may be, they were given as a means to life, not death. My times are in his hands, and nothing he has brought or allowed was meant to destroy, even those things that wounded deeply. His appearance on the shore that day in Galilee shouted, "I have come that you may have life," and his life-infusing presence makes my remembering a blessing, not a curse. So I'll stack my memories like stones, the way the children of Israel did as they crossed into the Jordan—some in the water, covered over by the river and never to be seen again, and some on the brand-new shore that waits for me. And I'll remember . . . that the surest things aren't foolproof. That the sweetest blooms have thorns. And that even the strongest of us can't make our heartfelt boasting stick, but he knows, and he loves us just the same.

The best remembering ends in praise. Remembering that you were lost, then found, is cause for rejoicing. Remembering that you were wounded, then healed, calls for songs of loudest praise. Remembering that you hungered and thirsted once upon a time makes even a crust of bread and a cup of water a banquet. "The pain then is part of the

pleasure now," a dying Joy Gresham said to her husband C. S. Lewis in the movie Shadowlands. Joy and sadness are even closer than we imagine. Memory connects them.

What's inside your "room called Remember"? Are there old addresses that you're afraid to revisit? Memories you've tried to banish that won't stay gone? Ask the One who's been to hell and back to take you by the hand and visit them again. You're safe now. They can't bully you anymore. There's a new King in town, and he bows to no one.

"Come, let us return to the LORD. For He has torn us, but He will heal us; He has wounded us, but He will bandage us. He will revive us after two days; He will raise up on the third day, that we may live before Him. So let us know, let us press on to know the LORD. His going forth is as certain as the dawn; and He will come to us like the rain, like the spring rain watering the earth" (Hosea 6:1–3).

"And Joshua said to them, 'Cross again to the ark of the LORD your God into the middle of the Jordan, and each of you take up a stone on his shoulder, according to the number of the tribes of the sons of Israel. Let this be a sign among you, so that when your children ask later, saying, "What do these stones mean to you?" then you shall say to them, "Because the waters of the Jordan were cut off before the ark of the covenant of the LORD; when it crossed the Jordan, the waters of the Jordan were cut off." So these stones shall become a memorial to the sons of Israel forever.' Thus the sons of Israel did as Joshua commanded, and took up twelve stones from the middle of the Jordan, just as the LORD spoke to Joshua, according to the number of the tribes of the sons of Israel; and they carried them over with them to the lodging place and put them down there. Then Joshua set up twelve stones in the middle of the Jordan at the place where the feet of the priests who carried the ark of the covenant were standing, and they are there to this day" (Josh. 4:5–9).

"Blessed are the poor in spirit, for theirs is the kingdom of heaven. Blessed are those who mourn, for they shall be comforted. . . . Blessed are those who hunger and thirst for righteousness, for they shall be satisfied" (Matt. 5:3–4, 6).

13

"You're Fired!"

The Ache of Labor

Work is not primarily a thing one does to live, but the thing one lives to do. It is, or should be, the full expression of the worker's faculties, the thing in which he finds spiritual, mental and bodily satisfaction.

Dorothy Leigh Sayers[1]

How many people do you know who are doing the thing they were made to do? "The place God calls you to," said Frederick Buechner, "is the place where your great love and the world's great hunger meet." But some of us labor years before we find that place, and some never seem to find it at all. The meanest ache of labor is not the ache that comes from tired muscles or taxed emotions or being spent for a grand cause or a small one. It's the ache of apathy, or boredom, or futility—of caring too little, for too long, for the very work that we've put our hand to.

I landed my first real job at thirteen, scoring Little League baseball for five dollars and a snow cone per game. It proved to be one of the most satisfying jobs I've ever had. I worked outdoors, and barefoot if I chose. The only equipment I needed was a lawn chair and a sharpened pencil. At the end of six innings or two hours, whichever came first, I had created a neatly penciled record of the game, giving me something tangible to show for my time. The only conflicts I experienced were with parents certain their son or daughter should not have been charged with an error or those who believed their offspring's fortunate arrival on base was the result of their own batting skill and not someone else's goofy mistake. (Kind of a no-win there; I always made someone unhappy, right or wrong.)

In my thirty years of work (counting that earliest start), I've been a scorekeeper, a drugstore cashier, a babysitter, a file clerk, a television news reporter, a publicist, a copywriter, an advertising account executive, a marketing director, a ghostwriter, an editor, and a freelance writer and consultant. I've been the "low man on the totem pole," and I've been the boss; I've been underpaid and overpaid, underappreciated and overrated, underutilized and in way over my head. The funny thing is, I never really meant to have a career at all.

Sometime around the launch of my scorekeeping gig, I believe, a member of my extended family asked me what I wanted to be when I grew up. Without hesitating or batting an eye, I answered, "Supported." After the laughter died down (I hadn't meant to be funny), I pointed out that "supported" seemed to work quite nicely for most of the grown-up women I knew, so I saw no compelling reason to break out of the mold.

Fate (or more likely providence) dictated otherwise. I graduated from college with a degree in journalism and discovered that liberal arts majors receive the lowest salary offers of any academic discipline. My first pay stub confirmed this sad statistic, but I managed to rent a small apartment, pay my bills, put gas in my car, and keep the pantry stocked with puppy chow and peanut butter. At first it actually seemed a little glamorous to be a "career girl."

For six years I hardly looked up. I did my best each day, angled for better assignments, and looked for opportunities to move up—and most of my friends were doing the same. We weren't so much compelled by what we *did* as we were concerned with *how we were doing*. We were striving to shape work lives that enhanced our image, or at least accessorized us well—not to find a good and true work in which to serve. The job was merely a means to an end for us; what end, we couldn't say. Movement mattered more than motive and title more than mission. And although we appeared to be in quite a hurry, it seemed then that we had more than enough time to get where we were going.

In my late twenties, I took a job for the first time for the money—and to get away from a supremely unhappy and unreasonable boss. I figured a job that paid nearly 30 percent more and wouldn't require me to swig from a Pepto-Bismol bottle several times a day *had* to be a good thing. It turned out to be more like jumping from the frying pan into the fire. My new boss had an especially volatile temper that he believed was simply the natural expression of "creative types," and he routinely stalked the halls of our shop slamming doors and screaming obscenities. (He had, however, been quite gracious and charming during my initial interview.) I took cover where I could find it and put all my efforts into my clients and my writing. I liked my co-workers a great deal but rarely chose to end the day with them in the tiny kitchen where they shared beers and battle stories until long after dark. I didn't mind that they drank and dished, but after eight to ten hours of "togetherness," I was ready to go home and lick my wounds . . . alone.

My future there was doubtless determined at my first evaluation, a year after I began my job as a copywriter and junior account manager. Facing my boss across the wide expanse of his oak desk and feeling a little like a girl called to the principal's office for a chat, I waited for him to take the lead. I didn't have to wait long. "Your work is very good," he said. "You're the best writer I have." I began to relax a little; maybe this wouldn't be too bad. "Your clients love you," he continued. "They can't say enough good things about you. And you get along great with your co-workers." He mentioned a handful of projects I'd participated in that had come off very well, lulling me into a false sense of well-being.

Then he switched gears. "But I don't get you at all," he said. "I know what makes Bob tick. I know what motivates him. I know what Bill's aspirations are and where he wants to go with the company. But you're a complete enigma to me. I have no idea what makes you tick." My already small confidence began to deflate like a helium balloon at a birthday party that had run too long. I wasn't sure where this was going, but it couldn't be anywhere good.

"I'm just not sure how you fit in here," he went on. "You never hang around for more than five minutes after all your work is done. You don't seem to have a real drive to grow the business or to invest yourself in this place." Here it was: my first lesson in office politics. And I had already failed the pop quiz without knowing I had taken it. I thought the point was to do good work, take care of my clients, and "play well with others," but I had obviously misread the unwritten how-to-get-ahead manual.

After the second half of his speech, I felt sure I was about to be dismissed. I couldn't imagine he still wanted me around after his summation of my disappointing work habits. But then he threw me another curve.

Slipping a piece of paper from underneath his legal pad, he folded it once and slid it across the big desk at me. "Here is your salary increase," he said. "It will be reflected on your next paycheck." My pride was still stinging from his previous words. I felt like an utter disappointment. Without thinking, I slid the piece of paper back across the desk, never glancing at the number inside. Then I summoned every shred of composure I still possessed and looked him straight in the eye. "If it's all the same to you," I said, "I'll just stay where I'm at. I'd rather get a raise when you feel like I've truly earned one." My act of idiocy rendered us both speechless. I stood, he stood, and I shook his hand and walked out. Two weeks later, my check reflected an increase, but not much of one. Whether it was the original number he had in mind or not, I did not know, but I knew this: No matter how good my work might have been, I was a misfit there. And he knew it too.

My annual review at the ad agency proved enlightening in the end. I decided that if passion was deemed just as important as actual job performance, I'd better find something to do that I was reasonably passionate about. And what I was most passionate about was God. So when a senior staff member of my church called a few months later and asked me to consider working there, I took her call as something of a sign. I wanted to do work that truly mattered and to impact something more meaningful than someone else's bottom line. My role as it was described to me would be to do creative work for the church, similar to what I was doing in the "secular" world. I would write, provide program support, plan special events, and promote them, all at a significant salary *decrease*. But I prayed over the decision, talked with others whose wisdom I valued, made myself a new budget, and said yes.

I no longer had just a job. I felt a genuine sense of calling. For the next ten years I labored in a beautiful vineyard, doing whatever I was asked and more. I stayed late. I went in early. I worked on weekends and holidays with people I truly loved and respected, and I became very good at what I did. And because I was doing "God's work," I never once questioned whether or not I was doing the work God had made *me* to do. I was safe, insulated, and caught up in the energy and momentum of a very large enterprise. I loved it so much I didn't notice for a decade that I'd lost myself somewhere along the way.

In her amazing essay "Why Work?" Dorothy Sayers wrestled brilliantly with the subject of work and vocation. "Work," she wrote, "should be looked upon as . . . a way of life in which the nature of man should find its proper exercise and delight and so fulfill itself to the glory of God." More than "a necessary drudgery to be undergone for the purpose of making money," Sayers deemed work "a creative activity undertaken for the love of the work itself" and "the full expression of the worker's faculties."[2]

For a long time I hadn't loved my work enough but even so expected far too much from it. For an even longer time I loved the nature of my work very much but paid no attention at all to my own true nature. I was well-used in a cause I cherished, but only so far as I forgot my own desires for the "greater good." I fit in by losing myself. The concepts of delight and God's glory hardly registered for me with regard to my gifts. I had no idea what the "full expression of my faculties" might look like. I may have even believed that if something delighted me, it wasn't very likely to bring any real glory and honor to the God I loved. Service and delight stood at cross-purposes for me. I ascribed to someone else's version of God's will for my life because I was afraid to discover it for myself.

In Matthew 25 Jesus told the story of a man about to go on a journey who called his slaves together to charge them with the care of his possessions. He did not divide the responsibility among them equally. To one he gave five "talents" or sums of money to invest, to another he gave two, and to another he gave one. The slaves who received five and two talents traded for even more, both doubling their original sums. But the slave who received a single talent feared losing what had been entrusted to him and buried the money in the ground. When the master returned, a full accounting ensued. The two slaves who doubled their master's talents were called "good and faithful" and given even more to manage. "Enter into the joy of your master," he told them (v. 21). But the poor, frightened slave who had buried his master's one talent was rebuked: "That's a terrible way to live! It's criminal to live cautiously like that! If you knew I was after the best, why did you do less than the least? The least you could have done would have been to invest the sum with the bankers, where at least I could have gotten a little interest. Take the thousand and give it to the one who risked the most. And get rid of this 'play-it-safe' who won't go out on a limb. Throw him out into utter darkness" (vv. 26–30 Message).

Two things about this story convicted me. First, each slave was responsible for what he had been given, not what someone else had been given. The assignments were individual—and the accounting was too. Second, the master valued the willingness to risk and rewarded it. He did not reward the man who, out of fear, merely played it safe.

I may have been more surprised than anyone when I left my safe and settled job on the church staff, but I knew it was time to discover what I had been given and to spend and grow what was entrusted to me, to my delight and to the glory of the Giver.

The longest playoff game in major league baseball history took place on October 9, 2005, and it matched my hometown team, the Houston Astros, against the visiting Atlanta Braves in the National League Central Division title series. This record-breaking contest will be remembered for many things, not the least of which is the fact that it lasted eighteen innings, or a grueling five hours and fifty minutes, and took the Astros almost every player on their forty-man roster to win. It was a demanding, beautiful, and very satisfying hard day's work.

In the bottom of the eighth inning, a grand slam home run by Astros outfielder Lance Berkman blew away a monstrous five-run lead by the Braves. An inning later, catcher Brad Ausmus tied it up with a two-out solo homer that sent the game into extra innings. Nine of them to be exact—although I stopped keeping score in the twelfth.

By the sixteenth inning, with seven pitchers spent and the bull pen drained, Astros manager Phil Garner looked down the bench to forty-three-year-old starter and future Hall of Famer Roger Clemens and nodded. Three days after throwing a ninety-three-pitch game, Clemens walked from the bull pen to the mound in only the second relief appearance of his legendary twenty-two-year career. Forty-four pitches and three scoreless innings later, he led the triumphant mob of players charging toward home plate to embrace rookie Chris Burke, whose game-winning solo homer barely cleared the short porch in left field.

"How can you not love the way that this guy plays and the preparation that he goes through?" asked starting pitcher Brandon Backe. "He just shut everybody down."[3] Clemens—a man clearly in love with his work—must have recognized his gifts early on, because he stewarded them well for more than half his life. He played his game fully and fearlessly, and I suspect never with more joy than in the sixteenth, seventeenth, and eighteenth innings of that epic game, serving in a role he could hardly be expected to fill. For the person who has found his place of service, "the work is the measure of his life, and his satisfaction is found in the fulfillment of his own nature, and in contemplation of the perfection of his work."[4]

I don't know what Roger Clemens believes about life and God and his glory, but watching him deliver pitch after game-hinging pitch near midnight with everything on the line reminded me of Olympic runner Eric Liddell's words, made famous in the movie *Chariots of Fire*: "When I run, I feel His pleasure." Clemens put in a full day "at the office." He (and thirty-seven of his teammates) left it all out there on the field, spending every last bit of what he had to give. Surely he must have felt no small amount of his Creator's pleasure in having done so.

When I left my job in ministry, I knew the next step would be a transitional one. I'd like to say I found my place immediately, but I didn't. I wasn't sure what "my place" looked like, so I returned to the corporate world. The money was quite good, but I had unknowingly stepped into a tumultuous situation, one that never righted itself over three years and four changes in leadership. When my fourth and final boss called me into her office during her third month, I knew what was coming. I'd been preparing myself for weeks.

Being "let go" in real life bears no resemblance to being voted off the island of Manhattan by Donald Trump à la *The Apprentice*. In the first place, the words "You're fired" are not generally spoken (especially not in our litigious society or in a situation where performance is not the issue). Instead, words like "restructure" and "rightsize" are used, along with polite assurances of how much your contribution was valued. In my case, the person doing the "rightsizing" read her remarks from a page of handwritten notes, and a human resources representative I'd never met sat next to me with a pre-typed severance agreement and a box of Kleenex. (Ironically, I'd never felt less like crying in my life.) As my new and soon-to-be former boss was speaking, my computer access was being terminated and the locks on my office door changed. (I'm still not sure what corporate secrets or supplies I was expected to make off with once I got the news.)

"I've never done this before," she said apologetically as she fumbled over her words. "That's okay," I told her. "I've never had this done to me, either, so we're in the same boat." When the formalities were dispensed with, she stood, shook my hand, and called me by the name of the next person on the list to be "rightsized," who was waiting just outside her door. She had four meetings in a row that afternoon; I suspect she was more ready than even I was to get home and call it a day.

I should have probably been at least a little frightened or sad or angry. But I wasn't. I felt almost buoyant. Relieved. God was calling me out of management and into mystery—but he had been faithfully preparing me to use the gifts he'd given and nurtured for so long. When I remarked to my older sister that for the first time in over twenty years I was not reporting to someone, she quickly corrected me: "Leigh, you're working for the same One you've always worked for. Nothing's changed." She was right.

I had always been held—but now it was finally time to fly. So I swallowed hard and began asking the question I should have been asking all along: "What would you have me to do today, God?" I didn't have a master plan, but I kept asking the question, and he kept answering it day by day. Sometimes my assignments resembled the kind of work I was used to. Sometimes they felt oddly like play. My working life became a series of little altars where I could go up in smoke and delight in doing so. I learned not to stammer when I called myself a writer. I had nowhere to take cover anymore but in the shadow of his wings. I have learned to love it there.

I office these days in the sunroom of my house. The windows face south to the tree-lined street, where the seasons change before my eyes. My neighbors wave as they come and go, and my dog lies near my feet. I never know where the next piece of work will come from, but it comes, and I receive it like manna with gratefulness and praise. I'm awed at the good things God brings my way. I am most definitely "supported"—but not in the way I thought I might be. It's even better than I imagined.

Painter Vincent van Gogh wrote in a letter to his brother Theo, "How can I be of use in the world? Cannot I serve some purpose and be of any good?" How right he was to ask those things. He sensed he was part of something big, and he knew how much pleasure he felt when he picked up a brush, pencil, or palette knife. "If you had only drawn one thing right," said van Gogh, "you would feel an irresistible longing to draw a thousand other things. I must go on . . . until my hand has become quite firm and my eye steady, and then I do not see any obstacle to my becoming quite productive."[5] Every right word I discover these days begs another and another. There is still so much to say, and so much more to learn.

My friend Karelyn paints in a light-filled flat in New York. Two of her paintings hang in my home, but many others are in much finer collections, exhibitions, and galleries. She has become an incredibly productive and gifted artist, but I treasure her friendship even more than her talent. She knows what it is to stand before a blank canvas and trust her gift enough to lift her brush and begin. Every day, in her studio or the classroom where she teaches, her offering goes up in smoke.

Denni cuts my hair every other month, but I would make appointments to see her even if she never picked up scissors again.

Her shop is a beautiful, warm sanctuary, and everyone who sits in her chair is loved and blessed. She is intense and alive and utterly focused on the person she is with. Every day she uses her gifts to the glory of the Giver.

Diane's office is elegant and gracious, like she is. It is the place where she gives herself away. The particulars of her job are coincidental—her field is friendship, and it is offered with love and faithfulness. Two chairs sit side by side with just enough space between them for her to look in your eyes and reach out and touch you. A small nosegay of Tootsie Pops are clustered in a crystal vase, just begging to be plucked. I have never found her door closed. Her heart is always open too.

This world is so hungry. Surely someone needs what it is in your nature to offer. What do you do that causes you to lose all track of time? Where do you most often experience delight, and when do you sense God's pleasure? Make an altar there, and climb on. You'll love how it feels to lose yourself in the sacrifice of a work well done . . . and God will be more than pleased to accept it.

"Whatever you do in word or deed, do all in the name of the Lord Jesus, giving thanks through Him to God the Father" (Col. 3:17).

"Whatever you do, do your work heartily, as for the Lord rather than for men; knowing that from the Lord you will receive the reward of the inheritance. It is the Lord Christ whom you serve" (Col. 3:23–24).

"On the contrary, who are you, O man, who answers back to God? The thing molded will not say to the molder, 'Why did you make me like this,' will it? Or does not the potter have a right over the clay, to make from the same lump one vessel for honorable use and another for common use?" (Rom. 9:20–21).

14

Lost Causes

The Ache of a Prodigal

The precious loses no value in the spending. A piece of hope spins out bright along the dark, and is not lost in space. Love is out orbiting, and will come home.

Luci Shaw

When someone or something you deeply value is lost, you cease to count the cost of restoration. You spend, even beyond your allotted budget of time or tears or treasure, in the hopes that your spending will pay off in the end. You keep on believing that tomorrow could be the day—that the next hour could be the one you've waited for—and you keep praying. Because to stop would be impossible . . . and because your God has proved over and over that his specialty is nothing less than impossible things.

*W*hat a difference a day can make! When the sun rose in the morning I was carefree and childless. When it set I had somehow opened my heart to a seventeen-year-old street kid I would come to love as if he were my son. If I had known then what the next eleven months would bring, I'm certain I would have wisely refused to become involved. And that would have been a terrible loss for both of us.

Sam[1] was a runaway teenager who needed help preparing for "emancipation"—a strange term for a boy turning eighteen with no family to take him in, no job, no driver's license, no high school diploma, and more unmatched baggage than an airport carousel could disgorge in a week's time.

The woman who phoned me and explained his situation apologized for even asking if I might be willing to help. "It looks pretty bleak," she confessed, "and I really don't know if there's much we can do for him." I stalled for time, telling her things I was sure she already knew: I was in the middle of a very busy season at work, had a serious writing deadline on top of that, and, as a single woman from an "all-chick" family, I knew hardly enough about teenage boys to fill a thimble. Surely there was someone better suited to the assignment than me?

She didn't disagree with any part of my argument, but when I was done she said this: "I completely understand. I do. But I called you because I knew if you took this kid on, you would pray for him . . . and he needs it." For the rest of the workday, I couldn't get Sam out of my mind. I read his file on my lunch hour, and the situation described on its pages quite literally terrified me. I would be utterly and completely out of my comfort zone from day one—and I knew it. But on the drive home, I began to pray, asking God for wisdom to make the right choice, even as I ordered my arguments to him against my saying yes.

Less than a hundred yards from my driveway, these words pierced my heart from out of nowhere: *"He is yours."* No, I didn't hear voices that day. I never have. But I knew. I just knew. And as disconcerting to me as the words were, I believed that to ignore them would prove even more risky. So I said yes to something I feared would change my life. And it did.

The first time Sam and I met was at a group home for boys not far from the neighborhood where I grew up. I had called ahead and told the resident director that I would be coming, and he told Sam to expect me. I knew a lot more about him that day than he knew about me, but those facts afforded me no comfort at all.

Sam had entered foster care when he was just a few months old. He hadn't seen his birth mother since that time; he did not know the identity of his biological father. In the interim years, his living situation had been only sporadically stable, and his behavior clearly reflected that. After running away and living on the street for many weeks, he had landed in an inner-city youth shelter, then in a psychiatric hospital. When he was released, no one who had previously cared for him was willing to take Sam in. The state placed him in the group home as a stopgap measure until he reached the legal age of adulthood.

The group home was a converted single-family residence in a sadly dilapidated state. It sat back on a large lot at the end of an unpaved, rutted driveway. A basketball goal with no net leaned awkwardly over the side patio, and a rusted weight bench stood outside the garage. The front door was sorely in need of paint, and a pane of glass was missing from the front window. I wasn't sure if the doorbell was operative, so I knocked loudly. The director I had spoken with answered within a few seconds. "I'll get Sam," he said as he directed me toward the living room sofa. When I sat down on it, I nearly sank through to the floor.

As Sam came in I stood and extended my hand. He looked momentarily confused, then offered his back in a weak hand-shake. I had braced myself for a big, tough-looking, angry kid. This boy was a tall, quiet waif who probably weighed less than 130 pounds soaking wet. His black hair was straight and thick and hung to just below his chin. His skin was a rich, exotic olive, and his eyes were deep brown. With a little creative art direction and better clothes, he could have been a hollow-cheeked, vacant-eyed blue jeans model in a fashion magazine spread. He flopped on the end of the couch, and I sat too, explaining why I had come and what I hoped we might accomplish together in the next few months. If he agreed (and he did, without protest), I would see him every week, and we would do what we could to get him ready to be on his own.

Before I left that day, I took a photograph of Sam, kneeling in front of the television set. He wasn't smiling, but his eyebrows were raised skeptically at me as if he were amused. I still have the photo. I left him a number where I could be reached, along with a spiral notepad and a couple of felt-tipped pens, and encouraged him to write down anything he wanted us to talk about the next time I came. I stayed less than an hour—the shortest visit we would ever have. I don't believe he thought I would be back. I couldn't understand how a boy like him had become so hopelessly alienated and lost. Or what I could possibly do to change that.

Lost things can consume your focus. A sheep or a coin, a boy or a dream, we spend inordinate amounts of time and energy seek-

197

ing to reclaim that which has been lost. Jesus spoke of lost things often, reminding his followers that while the cost of searching is often great, the joy of finding is ultimately greater. "Suppose one of you has a hundred sheep," he said, "and loses one of them. Does he not leave the ninety-nine in the open country and go after the lost sheep until he finds it? And when he finds it, he joyfully puts it on his shoulders and goes home. . . . I tell you that in the same way there will be more rejoicing in heaven over one sinner who repents than over ninety-nine righteous persons who do not need to repent" (Luke 15:4–7 NIV).

In Jesus's story, ninety-nine well-placed sheep were put at risk in order to find one straying one, because the straying one was at even greater risk. A sheep that had wandered away from the herd was vulnerable to attack by wild animals or likely to wander into a ravine or rocky crevice it could not easily get out of. Lone, wandering sheep were simply more prone to die. So the shepherd would trust the rest of the flock to protect itself while he went to rescue the wayward one. He would search until he found it—and when he did, he would place it lovingly upon his shoulders and carry it all the way home.

People get lost too. And when they do, those of us who love them become concerned for their safety. We worry and pray and use whatever resources we may have at the ready to find and restore our lost ones. Jesus knew that, and so he told a story that has become perhaps the most well-known and oft-told of all his parables. "There was a man who had two sons," he began, and then he quickly got to the conflict in his drama: "The younger one said to his father, 'Father, give me my share of the estate.' So he divided his property between them. Not long after that, the younger son got together all he had, set off for a distant country and there squandered his wealth in wild living" (Luke 15:11–13 NIV).

If Jesus's listeners that day had said to one another, "Nothing good can come of this," they would have been only partly right.

But like lost boy stories are wont to do, this one got ugly—very ugly—before it took a better turn. "After he had spent everything, there was a severe famine in the whole country, and he began to be in need. So he went and hired himself out to a citizen of that country, who sent him to his fields to feed pigs. He longed to fill his stomach with the pods the pigs were eating, but no one gave him anything" (Luke 15:14–16 NIV).

Almost every runaway reaches a point in his flight where garbage begins to look good . . . where perspective has become so skewed, where want and need are so sharply tuned, where desperation is so deeply felt that the prodigal truly believes that trash will satisfy him. Some call it hitting bottom. Some call it coming to the end of yourself. Any prodigal son or daughter remembers not just the day but the very moment of their darkest despair.

But in that watershed moment, something else is almost surely true. Someone, somewhere, has been waiting. Someone, somewhere, has prayed for just such a time. And someone, somewhere, long ago began the kind of lavish spending that every welcome home party worth its salt demands. The father in this story had surely trained his eye on the best calf in his herd, one he had not yet sold or slaughtered in hopes of just such a party. He must have gazed every morning and evening down the road by which he saw his youngest son depart, dreaming of the day it would be his boy's face—and not his back—that was indelibly etched in memory. And who could say how many tears were spilled or wordless prayers pushed heavenward on this lost one's behalf?

The neighbors probably talked. Neighbors often do. "He'll never be back," they likely said. "The old man's a fool to keep up that ridiculous road-watching vigil . . . and he was a fool to let him go to begin with."

Maybe so. But lost ones don't usually listen to reason. They've got a fire in their gut to wander—a gnawing unrest that won't let them wait for whatever good might one day be theirs. They go because they can't bear to stay another minute . . . but they are almost always gone longer than they need be.

Sam stole my heart away. He was not the son I had always wanted, but for nearly a year, he was the son-of-someone-else that I got, and he struggled at almost every turn. Academically he was far, far behind and had difficulty focusing on simple tasks. Spiritually a darkness surrounded him that I feared and prayed against with great diligence. Socially he was a misfit, and worse, he knew it. On the evening before his first day back in public school after a long stint in an alternative study environment, I asked him if he was feeling apprehensive.

"Yeah, kind of," he admitted.

"What makes you most worried?" I asked, thinking he might say "Algebra," or "English," or something else we might talk through together.

He hung his head and after a long time said, "What if no one lets me sit with them at lunch?"

I hadn't thought of that, but he had. And the uncertainty on his face when he choked out the words nearly undid me. I was beginning to understand what it must be like to be the parent of a wayward kid—and it hurt a lot more than I ever thought it might.

We had our ups and downs, Sam and me. But after a while he began to believe it when I said I would be there—that I wasn't leaving. He acted out to test me on it. Often. I went to school meetings and talked to counselors. I pushed for a better living situation and mediated disagreements. But mostly I showed up when I said I would, listened hard, and tried to offer him some of my hope.

At times his behavior was so outrageous and immature that I wanted to scream; he would say something so thoughtless or crude that I wished I could hide. After he had skipped school one day, breaking the explicit rules of the behavioral contract we had drafted together, he asked me if this latest infraction meant I was "through with him."

"What do you mean, 'through with you'?"

"I mean, are you going to quit coming around?"

"No, Sam, I'm not."

"Why not?"

"Because I love you, and because we have a deal."

"I don't know why you love me," he said. "No one else does."

I wasn't sure myself, but the words that came out next were wiser than me, and truer than I knew: "I love you because I've decided to and because when you're acting not-so-lovable, God helps me to."

There was a long silence on the other end of the phone.

"Oh," he finally said. "That's good."

Every time he got close enough to success to smell it, Sam acted out or sabotaged his own progress. Every time he began to let himself be comfortable with goodness, he felt the irrepressible urge to run, and most of the time, he did. There were periods of calm in between, but like every roller coaster, you knew what was coming after the climb. One Sunday in May, the phone rang.

"Hey," said Sam. "What are you doing?"

"Just got back from my parents' house, what about you?"

"Uh, nothing. I just called to wish you happy Mother's Day. I mean, you're not my mom or anything, but you're the closest thing I have right now. So . . ." He paused and I waited. He had run out of words.

"Thanks, buddy," I said. "I love you."

"Yeah, I know." Then his voice lowered to a whisper, as if he were afraid someone else might hear. "I, uh, love you too."

Three weeks later, he went missing. A week after that, he was found by the social worker assigned to him. As I hung up the phone after her call, I began making plans to visit Sam in a place I'd never been before: the county jail.

By this point my friends had begun to question my continued involvement, and my family had voiced more than a little concern about the heartbreak I had let into my life. But I wasn't counting the cost. For perhaps the first time ever, I wasn't running a balance sheet in my head. I was spending whatever resources I could muster—even ones I didn't think I had—because I wanted my lost sheep to be found. And not by me. By the only One who could safely carry him home.

The county detention facility was even worse than I expected. I cried the whole time I was there—so hard when I first saw him that I couldn't even speak. Sam looked at me through the glass that separated us and said over and over again, "I'm sorry. I'm sorry." I couldn't get my breath—it was as if someone had pounded me on the chest to restart my heart and then just kept wailing away. For the next few weeks Sam would spend his one phone call a day dialing my number. Each time I answered, an automated voice would ask if I would accept his collect phone call. We could speak for only a few minutes. I had more than a few minutes' worth to say, so I began to write and mail letters I was sure he probably read quickly, if at all, then just as quickly threw away.

When Sam was released over a month later and I picked him up, he had three things in the pockets of his baggy cargo pants: a bus token, a condom, and a handful of letters that had been folded and refolded so often they were falling apart.

I wish I could report that this lost sheep's story had a happy ending. I wish I could say that efforts made on his behalf resulted in a miraculous turnaround for Sam. They didn't and they haven't—but perhaps someday they may. Like the shepherd, my thoughts still linger on this missing one. Like the prodigal's father, I still watch the road and hope. I go to bed at night and pray that tomorrow I might hear some news, that tomorrow I might know he's made a way out of the even deeper hole he dug for himself. I spent a lot on Sam—and it looks for all the world like I spent for nothing. But I don't regret a minute of it, even though it crushed my heart. I believe I would spend just as liberally if I heard the words "he is yours" again. Because Sam wasn't just any lost cause. He was *my* lost cause. And I wasn't recruited to save him. I was recruited only to spend lavishly on his behalf.

The last letter I wrote probably never reached Sam. I still pray its words.

Do you still have the phone numbers I gave you? Are you ready yet to change your life? I love and miss you, but until you're ready to do something good for yourself, there's not much more I can do for you—except pray for you daily, which I do. Do you want to know what I pray, Sam? I pray this prayer from a poet named John Donne, who actually prayed it for himself—except when I pray, I put your name in it:

"O Lord, You have set up many candlesticks and kindled many lamps for my child, but he has either blown them out or carried them to guide him in forbidden ways. You have given him a desire of knowledge, and some means to it; but he has armed himself with weapons against You. Yet, O God, have mercy upon him. Let not his sin frustrate Your purpose in his life. But let him, in spite of himself, be of so much use to Your glory that by Your mercy other sinners may see how much sin You will pardon."

That may not make sense to you now, Sam—or you may not even care that you are prayed for. Matters not. You are.

When you are ready to make a change, I'm ready to support you and encourage you in it. You know where you need to start. I'll wait to hear from you.

Where is Sam now? I don't know. What difference did I make in his life? I can't say for certain. To the naked eye it doesn't look like my love made much of a dent at all. Here we spend lavishly without the certainty that our investment will pay off. Here we don't always get the delightful resolution that rings so joyfully true in the parable of the prodigal son. Here we fall asleep with doubts and nagging questions, and wake in the morning with no better answers than we had the night before.

If I didn't believe there was more, I might despair. If I thought I was the only one looking, praying, spending—I might give up. But I know better: "For this is what the Sovereign LORD says: I myself will search for my sheep and look after them. As a shepherd looks after his scattered flock when he is with them, so I will look after my sheep. I will rescue them from all the places they were scattered on a day of clouds and darkness. . . . I will search for the lost and bring back the strays. I will bind up the injured and strengthen the weak. . . . I will shepherd the flock with justice" (Ezek. 34:11–12, 16 NIV).

I know it's hard to believe, but it's true: Until this lost one disappeared, I had no idea how my own wanderings must have pierced the heart of God. But I do now. I know that his eye was trained on me and that he knew my whereabouts all along. I know he watched each wayward step and called to me in a voice that never stopped beckoning, pleading. Because he did so much for me, I wish I could have done more for Sam. I wish I had been wiser. I wish I had called sooner. Stayed on the phone longer. Asked more questions. Demanded more answers.

But more than anything, even today I wish to see my good Shepherd walking toward me, carrying on his shoulders the lost sheep I still love named Sam.

My generation is big on return-on-investment. We want to see results. We don't invest in much of anything at all unless we're relatively certain we'll be rewarded. But following the King into the mysteries of the kingdom may demand that we deny our rush to "cash in" and

introduce ourselves to the discipline of long, unmeasured spending. Some might call this lack of foresight. But not Jesus. He would call it faithful obedience—and he doesn't relent in asking for it.

Can you remember spending more of your time, money, energy, or love than felt comfortable because you believed God was calling you to do so? What did you discover in the process about yourself, your resources, and your God? Would you do it again if he asked? Is he asking now?

"But God, being rich in mercy, because of His great love with which He loved us, even when we were dead in our transgressions, made us alive together with Christ (by grace you have been saved), and raised us up with Him, and seated us with Him in the heavenly places in Christ Jesus, so that in the ages to come He might show the surpassing riches of His grace in kindness toward us in Christ Jesus" (Eph. 2:4–7).

"Be merciful, just as your Father is merciful. Do not judge and you will not be judged; and do not condemn, and you will not be condemned; pardon, and you will be pardoned. Give, and it will be given to you. They will pour into your lap a good measure— pressed down, shaken together, and running over. For by your standard of measure it will be measured to you in return" (Luke 6:36–38).

"We love, because He first loved us" (1 John 4:19).

Goodbye, Rhett Butler

The Ache of Grief

A picture needs a frame. A frame is its picture's friend. Death is our life's frame. That is how death is our friend.

Peter Kreeft, *Love Is Stronger than Death*[1]

"Good grief," Charles Schulz's cartoon character Charlie Brown frequently and plaintively muttered . . . but I wonder how many who've navigated grief have ever really thought to call it good. The universal response to loss is sorrow, and rightly so. But there is more. If we claim a Savior who's defeated death, then our most awful grief is only temporary. His coming, his death, and his resurrection really do "melt heaven and earth together, make death into sugar, and turn all ills, of which there are many, into delectable wine."[2]

*G*rief introduced itself to me when I was six and a speeding car struck our pet dachshund, Sugar Booger (no snickering, please: I didn't *name* him, I just loved him). My father gave the dog to my mother around the time I started kindergarten, so he was barely a year old when he died. I don't remember the accident or even being told by my parents that our family pet was gone . . . but I imagine they offered some explanation about him being in heaven and not able to return to us. I suspect this because the only memory I do have of the event is sitting on the steps of our front porch and begging my mother to let me go to heaven to see Sugar, then promising to come back home in time for dinner. (We hadn't learned the operating rules of the afterlife yet in Sunday school *or* Mrs. Johnson's kindergarten class.) Mother gently refused my plea, and I learned then that death means separation and that heaven, as near as it might seem, is not a destination easily accessed or temporarily visited.

I grieved for our lost dog the way a child grieves: desperately, tearfully, and rather quickly. I got over Sugar Booger's loss when we acquired another crazy dachshund named (more rationally) Fritz. Fritz lived a long, adventurous life before he too was felled by a passing car. Somewhere in between these two losses, the mean boy next door tossed our pet turtle down the driveway to its death, but I don't recall being sad about that so much as I was venomously angry at his little murderer.

No person I loved deeply died until I was eighteen and my father's mother quietly succumbed to a fatal heart attack, just moments after she had held her first great-grandchild in her arms. Grand Nona was a young sixty-six, so her passing was a shock. She died near Christmas, which she and my grandfather had celebrated in our home early that year so they could travel on to Oklahoma to see my cousin's new baby. My memories of that holiday with the two of them are still vivid. My parents gave them matching sandy-colored velour shirts as gifts, but they were mislabeled; she opened his and he opened hers, both exclaiming in delight at the confusion. I have a picture somewhere of her, sitting close to him, holding up his shirt and laughing.

Two other things stand out about my last days with her. For some unknown reason, she chose then to tell me the story of meeting my grandfather—a story she had never seen fit to share before. He had come to her home to pick up her twin sister for a date, but my grandmother opened the door instead, and the planned date never happened. They looked at one another and both immediately liked what they saw. My other Nona memory was of a kiss. My dad and I took them to the airport the day before Christmas, and at the terminal when she told me good-bye, she kissed me on the lips. I'm sure my grandmother had kissed me many times before, but this was a different kind of kiss—intentional and very deliberately and sweetly placed. The next day the phone rang with the news that she was gone. It was the first time I can remember seeing my father cry.

Again, the sting of death lies in its painful separation. Grand Nona had gone somewhere we couldn't travel, and her memory now had well-established borders. My recollection of her would forever stretch only as far back as I could remember and no further forward than the December day she died. Death had framed her, whole and complete. There would be no more to know of her, I thought, but in a strange way I was wrong.

Nearly twenty years later, sitting in a funeral home in Victoria, Texas, after my grandfather's death, an older couple approached my sister and me and introduced themselves. "You must be Sonny's girls," they said, and we nodded. (My father's name, like my grandfather's, is "Mac," but to him and my grandmother, my dad was always "Sonny.")

"We were friends of Mac and Nona's from Port Lavaca," they said. "We used to play cards together and go out on the boat fishing. We went dancing with them all the time." The cards part I could imagine; I'd often seen my grandparents play bridge. But my grandmother in a boat was a new image for me. Swimming, yes. Golfing, yes. But always beautifully manicured and impeccably outfitted. Grand Nona in a fishing boat was a picture that had never before presented itself to me. My elegant grandmother windblown on the bay seemed a genetic impossibility, but evidently it was not.

Then the couple sat down and proceeded to tell us stories of our grandparents not as we remembered them but as they were before we knew them. "We went out dancing with them one night," this couple said, "and your grandmother was wearing the cutest little flirty dress. Your grandfather couldn't take his eyes off of her, and he finally said with a smile, 'Nona, that dress is so small I could fold it up and put it in a matchbox.'" And as they told us story after story, my picture of my father's parents became sharper, clearer, and more lovely to me. Even more precious than their memory is the thought that, one day, I will see them both again and can ask about those sunny afternoons on the bay or the nights they went out dancing. Maybe then I'll know their favorite songs and their best fish tales and whatever happened to that little party dress—things I never thought to ask them when it seemed we had all the time in the world for storytelling.

Suffering and death bring with them a certain attentiveness that an endless string of days does not. They sharpen our focus on life and deepen our curiosity about its hidden drawers and corners. Facing our own death or experiencing the loss of someone we love is an awful, terrible ache . . . but an ache infused with the beauty of multifaceted memory and seasoned with the hope of a future, joyful reconciliation that will make this life's best moments pale in comparison.

When someone or something we love dies, grief opens our eyes more fully to life, as it did for Emily in Thornton Wilder's *Our Town*. She viewed Grover's Corners from the perspective of eternity: "Oh! Oh! It goes so fast. We don't have time to look at one another. . . . I didn't realize. So all that was going on and we never noticed. . . . Oh, earth, you're too wonderful for anyone to realize you. [She looks toward the Stage Manager and asks abruptly, through her tears] Do any human beings ever realize life while they live it?—every, every, minute?"[3] Philosopher Peter Kreeft says of death's life-sharpening value: "Why does death enhance life? Because it makes life scarce, and scarcity confers value. . . . Kill death and you will know the value of this friend. You will miss him when he is gone."[4]

We grieve more in this life than just physical death. The loss of a relationship stirs grief; so does the loss of innocence or the loss of hope. Dreams die hard, especially those we've held to longest, and the death of what might have been can prove just as painful as the death of what was. Any kind of deep loss rattles a double-edged sword. Before it arrives it inflicts fear or dread; after it departs it leaves a lingering residue of loss and longing in the wounds that it has made. Dying of any kind doesn't sit well with us. We were infused with eternity when we were conceived, just as inevitably as we were born into sin. We deserve death, yes . . . but we don't like it much at all.

My mother vowed after the deaths of our two dogs never to have another pet, but I made no such vow. So, soon after graduating from college and moving into my first apartment, I began looking for a dog. I didn't have to look far or long. One of the art directors at the ad agency where I worked announced that her parents' dog was expecting puppies. The mother was a black cocker spaniel; the father was a next-door neighbor's dog of unknown lineage. When the puppies were born, Cheri traveled to her parents' home in San Antonio and—in typical artist fashion—took Polaroid shots of each puppy and wrote notes about it on the back of the photo. I picked the only all-black male in the litter, the sweetest one of the bunch, Cheri said. When he was eight weeks old, I brought him home and named him Rhett Butler because he was dark and handsome and I loved Clark Gable in *Gone with the Wind*.

Rhett became an instant companion. When he was small I used to carry him in a basket, like Dorothy carried Toto in *The Wizard of Oz*. He knew my secrets, protected my apartment with the fierceness of a dog three times his size, and slept like a baby at the foot of my bed. He saw me through the ups and downs of early adulthood and was even, as it turned out, an excellent judge of men. (It took me longer to learn to discern character as quickly and as well.) Probably because of the tragic ends of the only other two dogs I remembered, I never let Rhett venture outside off of his leash. He lived safely and happily, with only one near-death experience, which resulted from his consumption of several ounces of chocolate chips in a huge hurry when my back was turned.

Rhett lived fourteen years before his health visibly worsened. He began to sleep longer and eat less frequently. When I took him outside, he seemed confused about what to do, tiptoeing about as if the ground were some sort of strange lunar surface, not St. Augustine grass. He began to have housebreaking "lapses" with alarming frequency. Normally a very affectionate animal, he no longer tolerated being petted or held. He stayed underneath the kitchen table or my bed for hours and had to be coaxed out. Seeing him in such decline was heartbreaking. I had not lived alone for more than a few weeks without him, and I was devastated at the thought of losing him but unwilling to let him suffer needlessly. I made an appointment with his veterinarian, a kindly man I'd known since I was eight years old. If Rhett was to be put to sleep, I wanted to make the arrangements *before* the dreaded day came. I needed to be ready.

Dr. Wright greeted me with a cheerful smile and said, "Let's talk." I explained the problems Rhett was having, and he gently said that my dog's behavior was typical of animals nearing the end of life. We talked about whether or not he was suffering and how I would know when it was time. Then I steeled myself and asked the hard stuff that I felt I needed to know. How, exactly, were animals put to sleep? How long did it take? What did they feel? How were their remains disposed of?

Rhett would receive two shots, Dr. Wright explained—the first an injection to relax him and make him drowsy, the second a dose strong enough to stop his breathing in seconds. Some people dropped their pets off, Dr. Wright said, and others held them while they were euthanized. As much as I wanted to be a drop-off kind of girl, I knew that I was not. I couldn't bear the thought of handing him over to someone at the door and walking away. Although I hoped that Rhett would simply fall asleep one night and not wake up, I paid that day for the thing that I was dreading so that if I had to bring Rhett to be euthanized, I wouldn't have to write a check in exchange for his death. Dr. Wright hugged me, and I went home to the vigil.

Rhett lingered. He grew weaker by the day, but he would still raise his head when I came home and drink a little water. One morning when I woke, he was lying on a pair of jeans I'd tossed on the floor the night before, and he had soaked them through with urine. He didn't raise his head or move at all—just looked at me with his beautiful dark eyes. I knew. I called and made the appointment. It was the only thing left to do.

My parents, who had grown to love the dog almost as much as I did, offered to take him so that I wouldn't have to, but I couldn't allow it. I knew it would be just as awful for either of them, and besides, he was my responsibility. I was a grown-up now. Rhett was mine to hold, even to the end. My boss at the time made the same kind offer, but the thought of passing him off to a near stranger felt even worse. I called a dear friend and asked her to come with me, and she graciously agreed.

Diane and I made our way to Dr. Wright's in near silence. I drove, and Rhett lay in my lap. I carried him in; he was too weak to walk. We were ushered in back almost as soon as we arrived, and Dr. Wright explained again what he would do. I placed Rhett on the cold steel table and encircled him with my arms. He closed his eyes after the first shot was administered, but his breathing remained steady and regular. Dr. Wright asked if I was ready for him to give the second injection, and I nodded yes. My arms were still wrapped around Rhett's frail form, and silently, Diane wrapped her arms around my waist from behind and pressed her cheek against my shoulder. My tears were falling unchecked on the table. Dr. Wright's eyes were wet too. He warned that Rhett might jerk or shudder with the final shot, but he did not. He barely moved, and I laid my face against his ribs and listened as his breathing stopped and his heart stilled. Just like that, in seconds it was done. My sweet companion of fourteen years was not going home with me. I unbuckled his collar and slid it from around his neck. Then I kissed the warm head of my well-loved pet and said, "Goodbye, Rhett Butler." It was the only time in my life I had watched death come and go with my own eyes.

The emptiness of my house that night was excruciating. Even when sick, Rhett had been so much a part of my everyday existence that his absence left a huge, gaping hole. I left his food and water bowls, clean and untouched, on the kitchen floor for nearly a month before I could bear to put them away. The words "Good Dog" were painted on the inside of one of them. He most surely was.

Grieving is an incredibly inefficient process. It sets its own pace and seldom bothers to announce its comings and goings. Tears spring up unexpectedly, just when we think we've mastered our emotions. Memories surface at inconvenient times. Some of us are "graveyard" people; some of us are not. Some need physical reminders of the thing that was lost; others shun such things. Some of us hurry through our grief; others linger longer than perhaps we think they should. But who can say, really, how to navigate such unknown waters? Each of us must find our own way, but thankfully, we do not do so alone.

She had watched him die. Many of his followers stopped short of his final destination: a hill on the outskirts of the city of Jerusalem where common criminals were executed. The placard above his head said "King of the Jews," and maybe he was. But however far the borders of his kingdom did or did not extend, she could say for certain that they included her own heart.

Because she knew where they had laid his body, she returned to that place on the first day of the week, wanting to be near him as she grieved. Only when she arrived she discovered the tomb standing open, unsealed. She ran for his disciples Simon Peter and John and begged them to return to the spot with her: "They have taken away the Lord out of the tomb, and we do not know where they have laid Him," she said (John 20:2). Peter ran ahead and burst into the tomb. The linen wrappings that had surrounded Jesus were inside, but he was not. The men surveyed the situation, not comprehending what had happened. They saw nothing there to be done, so they returned home. But Mary did not. She stayed.

Can you imagine a sorrow deeper than this? She had loved him completely and seen the very life drain out of him before her eyes. He was her hero, her rescuer, her friend. And now he was lost. The story that had looked so promising had gone tragically awry, sealing off her hopes as permanently as his body had been sealed two days before. But now his tomb was empty. What to make of this? Where was he? The Gospel of John records what happened next:

> But Mary was standing outside the tomb weeping; and so, as she wept, she stooped and looked into the tomb; and she saw two angels in white sitting, one at the head and one at the feet, where the body of Jesus had been lying. And they said to her, "Woman, why are you weeping?" She said to them, "Because they have taken away my Lord, and I do not know where they have laid Him." When she had said this, she turned around and saw Jesus standing there, and did not know that it was Jesus. Jesus said to her, "Woman, why are you weeping? Whom are you seeking?" Supposing Him to be the gardener, she said to Him, "Sir, if you have carried Him away, tell me where you have laid Him, and I will take Him away."

> John 20:11–15

Then the unthinkable: "Jesus said to her, 'Mary!' She turned and said to Him in Hebrew, 'Rabboni!' (which means, Teacher)" (v. 16).

She believed she stood alone in her grief. She did not. Not only did Mary not grieve alone, she grieved in the very presence of the only One whose power could mitigate her pain. And so do we. The arms of my friend wrapped around me as my sweet pet breathed his last were a tangible reminder of the presence I can count on when my heart is past breaking. And in the presence of this One, the worst that could happen can be transformed into the best that could ever be. The end of one good thing can become the beginning of a far greater one. Sorrow can be made into joy, and tragedy into triumph.

Because Jesus took on the worst the world could offer, because he drank fully the cup that kills, died in shame, and rose in victory, our griefs are forever transformed. And because the One who loved us first and best reaches past our pain and calls our name, we can be sure there is more beyond our sorrow. In the presence of the Beautiful One, our grief becomes precious too.

Do you have a grief of your own that demands attention? Have you believed that by ignoring it you can make its ache go away? You cannot. But by inhabiting it and discovering there the presence of the living Christ, it may be transformed. Sorrow is exactly the sort of setting that showcases his mercy, and his fellowship in the midst of grief truly does, in Luther's words, "make death into sugar" and our most awful heartaches into "delectable wine."

Because Jesus has defeated our ultimate enemy, the death penalty—or any smaller charge against us—simply cannot "stick." Jesus's death and resurrection has left Satan and his attending sorrows about as scary and impotent as a four-foot-tall, trick-or-treating Frankenstein. We can live dying, grieving every loss as if it were the final word, or die living, letting the resurrected One transform our grief into something indestructible and fine. The choice is ours. But the victory will be forever his.

"Father, I desire that they also, whom You have
given Me, be with Me where I am, so that they may

see My glory which You have given Me, for You loved Me before the foundation of the world. O righteous Father, although the world has not known You, yet I have known You; and these have known that You sent Me; and I have made Your name known to them, and will make it known, so that the love with which You loved Me may be in them, and I in them" (John 17:24–26).

"Sing praise to the LORD, you His godly ones, and give thanks to His holy name. For His anger is but for a moment, His favor is for a lifetime; weeping may last for the night, but a shout of joy comes in the morning" (Ps. 30:4–5).

"The righteous cry, and the LORD hears and delivers them out of all their troubles. The LORD is near to the brokenhearted and saves those who are crushed in spirit. Many are the afflictions of the righteous, but the LORD delivers him out of them all" (Ps. 34:17–19).

"Lo, I am with you always, even to the end of the age" (Matt. 28:20).

16

Singing the Hymnal

The Ache to Worship

A lightning flash, my pounding heart
A breaching whale, a shooting star
Give testimony that you are
And my soul wells up with hallelujahs.

Chris Rice, "Hallelujahs"[1]

C. S. Lewis said that the praise of a thing is the natural and satisfying end of its appreciation. When we experience something especially fine, we want to make its excellence known—and our enjoyment of it is never truly complete until we've done so. Whether that thing is a perfectly prepared recipe, a grand-slam home run, or a sleeping newborn, we're strongly compelled to praise its goodness. We are people made to praise . . . and we will surely do it, lauding lesser objects until the finest One is found.

There are 553 hymns in the old hymnal on my bookshelf, counting the "amens" and the "benedictions." I know at least half of them by heart—maybe more if I could hear the organ prelude to those tunes I can't quickly summon from memory. This is by no means a boast. I have never set out to memorize even a single one of them. But hymns were the assembled soundtrack of my childhood, and they sank in deep.

My sister, my cousin, and I performed "Love Lifted Me" for our parents in a back bedroom concert once, coming out of the double-doored walk-in closet onto the carpeted "stage" like Johnny Carson parting the curtain at NBC. (I believe we also sang a little Sinatra and "America the Beautiful" in the same gig.) "This Is My Father's World" was the first hymn whose words I learned beginning to end, the summer before my third-grade year. To this day, the first few notes of it coax a silent smile and an acknowledgment that it is, indeed, *still* his world.

I learned to praise God before I knew him for myself—but secondhand knowledge proved a good enough tool with which to begin. Hymn number one in our book was "Holy, Holy, Holy," teaching me that his holiness was but one of the attributes that made God special. The invitational hymn at the end of any sermon would likely be "Just as I Am," or "I Surrender All," or "The Nail-Scarred Hand," and by them I discovered that God's kind overtures invite our clear response. Fanny Crosby, Charles Wesley, and Isaac Watts provided my first exposure to pure poetry (Dr. Seuss and nursery rhymes excluded), and I adored their words, even when I didn't fully understand them. When we sang Fanny's

"Tell Me the Story of Jesus," I too was asking God to "write on my heart every word," and learning that "love paid the ransom for me."[2] Salvation hymns like "I Am Resolved" repeatedly assured me that "He is the true one, He is the just one, He hath the words of life."[3]

I held on to one half of the hymnal then, reaching up for it with my mom or dad's hand reaching down to steady the other side. For reasons that are still a mystery to me, we routinely skipped the third verse of each hymn, and we overlooked the "Holy Spirit" hymns almost entirely. (While he may have been an acknowledged equal in the Godhead, where I grew up, the Holy Ghost was the least-referenced member of the Trinity, hands down.) We were much less squeamish about the "blood" hymns, though, singing at least one of them a week. Scary movies were strictly taboo, but no one bothered to shield my youthful innocence from that "sacred head now wounded" or the broken, dying Savior who "groaned upon the tree."

When, at age eight, I slipped out of my pew with my parents and walked the aisle of the church to declare I had given my heart to Jesus, the grown-ups around me were singing "Call—ing to-day, Call—ing to-day, Je—sus is call——ing, is ten-der-ly call-ing to—day."[4] And so he was—as much, I suspect, through the messages of the hymns as through any preaching or teaching I had heard and understood. So it was only natural, I suppose, that the music that first anchored me to God would be the music I most often used to praise him. My appreciation of his goodness truly *was* enlivened by singing of it, and my gratefulness for his mercy was too.

Even today, when I yearn to feel his presence, I'm just as likely to sing "Come, Thou fount of every blessing" as I am to whisper "Dear Lord . . ." Words to hymns are regularly scrawled on the wall-sized blackboard hanging in my dining room, jumbled there with the odd dinner menu, contemporary song lyrics, a snippet of Elizabethan poetry, or a stray line from Bono's quirky, piercing pen. Thus posted, these words quickly remind me that "There are depths of love that I cannot know / Till I cross the narrow sea; / There are heights of joy that I may not reach / Till I rest in peace with Thee."[5] Like Annie Dillard, I know only enough of God to want to worship him by any means close to hand. And because the hymns are close—to my hand and my heart—I find myself reaching for them often when I feel the overwhelming need to offer him my praise.

When God sought to give specific instructions to his people, he began by addressing their propensity to worship. He knew the human heart—why wouldn't he? He created it! He knew well this desire of ours to bow down, to shout out, to extol and honor and glorify. He also knew our temptation to squander our praise on lesser things. So he began his commandments to his children with this primary one: "I am the LORD your God, who brought you out of the land of Egypt, out of the house of slavery. You shall have no other gods before Me. You shall not make for yourself an idol, or any likeness of what is in heaven above or on the earth beneath or in the water under the earth. You shall not worship or serve them; for I, the LORD your God, am a jealous God" (Exod. 20:2–5).

What need would there have been for such a prohibition if man were not prone to worship? Why the stern warning if praise were not hardwired into us somehow, just waiting for the appropriate object to commandeer its expression? When God is not the recipient of our praise, we don't stop praising . . . we just redirect our wonder. We roar for sports heroes, wait in line to see matinee idols, watch red carpets, and sight stars, awed at the extraordinariness of mortals just like us, only "better." We rise to our feet in concerts and strain to catch a glimpse of performers who stand no closer than we do to the truly transcendent. And God knew that we would. So he gave us the one eternal thing that exists that can never be praised long or loudly enough, that can never get all the glory it deserves: He gave himself.

Imagine a handful of country shepherds on a hillside in Judea. The night sky is full of stars, and their bellies are full from dinner. The sheep are beginning to settle in for the night and are finally quiet. The shepherds themselves are looking for a smooth, flat place to lie down so that they can both nap on and off and keep an eye on their flocks spread out beyond.

Then all heaven breaks loose.

An angel comes to stand before them, shimmering and bright. A light show such as they'd never seen commences. The sheep begin to panic and bleat, confused and running this way and that. The shepherds are confused too, and frightened. "The glory of the Lord shone around them," the story goes, and then the angel spoke good news: "For today in the city of David there has been born for you a Savior, who is Christ the Lord" (Luke 2:9, 11). The shepherds found the announcement so stunning that they decided to go and see for themselves: "Let us go straight to Bethlehem then," they said, "and see this thing that has happened which the Lord has made known to us" (Luke 2:15).

There they found Mary, Joseph, and Jesus, just as the angel had said, and returned to their fields "glorifying and praising God for all that they had heard and seen" (Luke 2:20). These ordinary herd-watchers couldn't keep it in. They were changed men. Nothing would be the same after that. They had found the One worth worshiping and given him their praise.

Now fast-forward thirty-three years. The baby announced that night is now a man, and in just days he will die for the sins of the world. But this night he is together with friends, eating and drinking. Two sisters of Lazarus were there: Mary and Martha. Martha was serving the dinner, but Mary was not; she was lingering at the edges of the meal and the conversation, listening to Jesus talk and wanting to be near him. She was holding something in her hands. And waiting. Finally, when she could be still no longer, she moved forward with a container of costly perfume, and in full sight of all she broke it and poured it over his feet in a gesture of love and honor. (If that wouldn't grind a dinner party to a halt, can you imagine what would?)

As the rich fragrance filled the hushed room, Mary knelt before Jesus and wiped the perfume into his feet with her hair. What she did was extravagant. It was an interruption. It appeared intimate and perhaps even embarrassing to others in the room. But those things never mattered to Mary. The object of her affection had summoned her worship—and she had responded with whatever means she had at hand. She couldn't *help* but worship him. If she had not, the unbroken container would have mocked her every time she looked at it. It was meant for him . . . and she surely knew it.

Even so, some objected. One of Jesus's disciples decried it as a shameful waste: "Why was this perfume not sold for three hundred denarii and given to poor people?" (John 12:5). But the object of this lavish praise did not object. He told the protesters to leave Mary alone and said that she should keep what perfume remained for the day of his burial, hardly a week away. "For you always have the poor with you," he explained gently, "but you do not always have Me" (John 12:8).

More than she needed the approval of others, more than she needed to appear dignified and discreet, more than she needed to save up a treasured supply of rich perfume, Mary needed to demonstrate her love for Jesus. That love spilled out of her just as surely as her precious perfume spilled onto the feet of her

Lord and its fragrance permeated the very air of the room. She was made for praise, and she had found the One who should receive it. It would have been easier to stop breathing than to let the moment pass without giving him his due.

My friends and I have a code term for full-out, facedown worship. We call it "the Father Ralph," so named for the scene in the movie *The Thorn Birds* where Father Ralph de Bricassart is ordained to the priesthood, lying prone on the chancel floor in the distinct shape of a cross. We make light of it the way convicted felons must joke about death row: fully aware that this sort of thing is no laughing matter but grasping for the tiniest scrap of levity to steel ourselves against its awful weight. "It is a terrifying thing," said the writer of Hebrews, "to fall into the hands of the living God" (Heb. 10:31). No doubt he knew of what he spoke.

Real praise—true worship—is more than an inward acknowledgment. Our bodies are commissioned to the endeavor just as much as our souls. The shepherds got to their feet and traveled to be in Christ's presence. Mary moved forward in a crowded room and quite literally threw herself at Jesus's feet. We're called and compelled to present our bodies, as Paul says, "a living and holy sacrifice, acceptable to God" so that our worship might be serviceable (Rom. 12:1). We offer lip service, sure. But he merits far, far more than that.

Audiences at sporting events or performances don't sit silently by and watch. They applaud. They rise to their feet. They employ their voices in rebel cries or dignified "bravos" or cheers. They do the "tomahawk chop" or the wave. They stamp their feet and pump their fists in the air. They go full out. They get into it. The compelling desire to praise God is so strong that if we don't do it, Jesus said, inanimate things may well pick up our slack: "As

He was going, they were spreading their coats on the road. As soon as He was approaching, near the descent of the Mount of Olives, the whole crowd of the disciples began to praise God joyfully with a loud voice for all the miracles which they had seen, shouting, 'Blessed is the King who comes in the name of the LORD; Peace in heaven and glory in the highest!' Some of the Pharisees in the crowd said to Him, 'Teacher, rebuke Your disciples.' But Jesus answered, 'I tell you, if these become silent, the stones will cry out!'" (Luke 19:36–40).

It was nearing midnight in the isolated cabin I'd rented, and only the oil lamps still offered light. The fire that had whooshed and cracked and popped just an hour before burned now with only a faint orange glow. I had begun the evening in a warm, comfortable chair, wrapped in a blanket and listening to music on my portable player. But I wasn't making any music, and as much as the words echoed the cry of my heart, they weren't *my* cry.

Slipping the earbuds out, I put the device away, laid my head back, and began to sing from the beginning of an unseen hymnal—starting with hymn number one: "Holy, holy, holy, Lord God Almighty! Early in the morning my song shall rise to Thee; Holy, holy, holy, merciful and mighty! God in three persons, blessed Trinity."[6] Then song by song, line by line, the words came flooding out: "Be Thou my vision, O Lord of my heart; Naught be all else to me, save that Thou art: Thou my best thought, by day or by night; Waking or sleeping, Thy presence my light. Riches I heed not, nor man's empty praise; Thou mine inheritance, now and always: Thou and Thou only, first in my heart, High King of heaven, my treasure Thou art."[7] From "Come Thou Fount" to "There Is a Fountain," from "He Leadeth Me" to "Lead On O King Eternal," from "My Jesus I Love Thee" to "I Love to Tell the Story," I sang on and on until my voice was a hoarse croak and no more lines came.

And it wasn't enough.

So I climbed from my chair and crouched before it on my knees, pressing my face into the soft corduroy of the seat cushion and feeling my own warm breath coming back at me. Bowed there I said his name over and over.

But it still wasn't enough.

Then, because no one else could see, I crawled before the fire and lay facedown, spread into the shape of his cross and feeling every inch of the cold floor against my chin and ribs and belly and knees and feet. It was better. But it still wasn't enough. There weren't enough hymns to praise him with. Not enough words to whisper in prayer. I couldn't get low enough to show him my gratitude or stay there long enough to express my devotion. There simply hadn't been enough to praise him with. And I ached for more. "Everything about life in this world is meant to leave us redemptively discontent," says pastor Scotty Smith. "We aren't home yet. Even what we would call the best worship service imaginable is meant to make us restless for perfect worship, which will only be celebrated after the return of Jesus, Bridegroom for Bride."[8]

We were made to worship. Made to praise. And one day, we will do it to our hearts' content. We will discover the words to a new, satisfying song—and maybe realize that it was in us all along. We will sing music such as this world has never heard, together with a chorus of billions of voices—voices of angels and voices like our own. And the beautiful object of that rightly placed worship—our King—will be near enough to touch and as visible to us as this morning's sunrise. Best of all, we will have forever to keep on getting it right, never at a loss for words.

Would you like a preview? It will look something like this:

Behold, a throne was standing in heaven, and One sitting on the throne. And He who was sitting was like a jasper stone and a sardius in appearance; and there was a rainbow around the throne, like an emerald in appearance. Around the throne were twenty-four thrones; and upon the thrones I saw twenty-four elders sitting, clothed in white garments, and golden crowns on their heads. Out from the throne come flashes of lightning and sounds and peals of thunder. And there were seven lamps of fire burning before the throne, which are the seven Spirits of God; and before the throne there was something like a sea of glass, like crystal; and in the center and around the throne, four living creatures, full of eyes in front and behind. . . . And the four living creatures, each one of them having six wings, are full of eyes around and within; and day and night they do not cease to say, "Holy, holy, holy is the Lᴏʀᴅ God, the Almighty, who was and who is and who is to come." And when the living creatures give glory and honor and thanks to Him who sits on the throne, to Him who lives forever and ever, the twenty-four elders will fall down before Him who sits on the throne, and will worship Him who lives forever and ever, and will cast their crowns before the throne, saying, "Worthy are You, our Lord and our God, to receive glory and honor and power; for You created all things, and because of Your will they existed, and were created."

Revelation 4:2–6, 8–11

One day we will have whatever we need to praise him "close to hand," and there—for the first time and forever—that praise will satisfy us in a way that this world's best hallelujahs could not. "O that with yonder sacred throng we at His feet may fall! We'll join the everlasting song, and crown Him, Lord of all."[9]

Some things leave you speechless. Seeing Michelangelo's David *in the pure light of the Academy in Florence, Giotto's frescoes on the walls of the chapel of St. Francis in Assisi, and the aspens flaming yellow high above the tiny town that bears their name—all of these have stolen my faculty for words. But so have a single star seen from my back stoop and the long pull of a bow across the strings of a cello. When I see and hear these things, I know that they are nothing more than the jumbled notes of an orchestra tuning itself for eternity. And as hard as I try, I can't imagine what that music will do to my weak, unpracticed voice.*

What evokes praise in your heart? Can you see or hear or discern in those things the hint of something vastly bigger, greater, and wilder? Would you dare to begin to honor it now, today, knowing that even incomplete hosannas are a reasonable man's best method of practice?

"The LORD is my strength and song, and He has become my salvation; this is my God, and I will praise Him; my father's God, and I will extol Him" (Exod. 15:2).

"Then I looked, and I heard the voice of many angels around the throne and the living creatures and the elders; and the number of them was myriads of myriads, and thousands of thousands, saying with a loud voice, 'Worthy is the Lamb that was slain to receive power and riches and wisdom and might and honor and glory and blessing.' And every created thing which is in heaven and on the earth and under the earth and on the sea, and all things in them, I heard saying, 'To Him who sits on the throne, and to the Lamb, be blessing and honor and glory and dominion forever and ever.' And the four living creatures kept saying 'Amen.' And the elders fell down and worshiped" (Rev. 5:11–14).

"For here we do not have a lasting city, but we are seeking the city which is to come. Through Him then, let us continually offer up a sacrifice of praise to God, that is, the fruit of lips that give thanks to His name" (Heb. 13:14–15).

A Table in the Wilderness

The Ache to Feast with God

I am my beloved's and my beloved's mine
so you bring all your history
and I'll bring the bread and wine
and we'll have us a party where all the drinks are on me
then as surely as the rising sun you will be set free.

Derek Webb, *Lover*[1]

Too many of us fritter our lives away waiting for the next big payoff. For the ultimate job, or the perfect holiday; for graduation day, or a wedding day; for opening nights, or birthdays, or the first day of summer. We yearn for the day that our hopes will be fulfilled, our efforts rewarded, our struggles explained, and our hungers satisfied. What we too often miss is this: God is at work all along the way. He is arranging little celebrations in between the ones we've scheduled and inviting us to feast like the sons and daughters we already are while his party-to-end-all-parties is being made ready.

As a little girl, I made elaborate mental lists of all the things I was looking forward to that had not happened yet. At any given point my list might include a friend's birthday party, a field trip to the zoo, a book I hadn't read but wanted to, or an episode of a favorite television program I had not yet seen. And in a strange way I can't really explain, reviewing my "not yet" list never failed to give me joy. There was also, along with the joy, a fleeting pang of longing or anticipation that was not entirely without its ache. But it never made me sad to think of these just-out-of-reach things. Instead it gave me pleasure.

Apparently I was not alone. Once when my youngest niece was eight or nine and we were sitting in the paper-littered aftermath of another embarrassingly bountiful Christmas, she looked at me (over her eye-high stack of gifts) and said with a plaintive sigh of regret, "I wish it wasn't Christmas." Thinking her haul had been pretty generous and imagining that I personally would have been delighted with it, I asked her why she would say such a thing. "Because it's just so much fun to look forward to," she said with a shrug.

I can't pinpoint the age that my list of pending delights was quietly retired, but this much I confess: The shift from open longing to quiet resignation has mostly lacked that early whiff of joy. The things I thought at twelve were a near certainty are not so easy to maintain optimism for thirty years hence. And although it's blatantly bad form to question the God who provided manna in the wilderness, I sometimes wonder if the Israelites, traveling in such a large group, might not have been easier for him to spot and hence to bless.

All my dreams have not come true—even some of the ones I've most longed for. And I've followed my God a long way down the road. I've never openly denied him, or taken a self-proclaimed "church holiday," or shirked my duty, or turned my back on his claims. I taught Sunday school for sixteen years straight because I was asked to, and I skipped the unpredictability of the weekly offering plate in favor of direct deposit giving. In some ways I'm still checking the row of boxes that ran along the bottom of my offering envelopes as a child: *Present, Lesson Studied, Offering Brought, Bible Read*. If only it were that straightforward: fifty cents a week and an envelope with four penciled checkmarks. But it's not. Not even close.

Once, when I was fresh out of school and on a business trip to Florida, I gave serious consideration to taking a break from self-imposed piety and tasting some of the more alluring things that the world seemed to offer. God hadn't "delivered the goods," so why not?

I was, after all, in a strange place with people who didn't know whose I really was. But I knew. And as much as I thirsted for freedom and adventure and acceptance and the fleeting buzz of complete and total irresponsibility, *I* couldn't forget. So, alone on my knees in a beautiful condo on a moonlit beach at nearly 3:00 in the morning, I prayed this not-so-spiritual prayer: "Okay, God, I guess it's going to be you and me, since you've ruined me for anything else. I can't get the things I want the way the world gets them and be happy about it. So I'm yours. You've got my life. I hope you're satisfied with it."

I'm not particularly proud of that moment, watershed though it was. If sliding halfheartedly into sin had been any easier, I very likely would have done it. But I didn't want the things I wanted as much as I wanted for my wants to be supplied by my great and good God—and to be glad in him and also in them. I wanted to have my cake and eat it too. I still do.

Were I to read these words as an unbiased observer, I'd say that their writer has a somewhat stunted view of grace. That she seems awfully works-oriented. That it's no wonder she's not feeling much joy. And I'd venture her estimation of her own performance is probably overly generous.

Fair enough.

I *haven't* learned as much as I should or trusted as fully as I might—and if the cup of my life looks comparatively clean on the outside, I'm not fool enough to think that a peek inside the rim would impress my neighbors, my enemies, *or* my God. Far from it.

The fact that I haven't yet resorted to a kind of do-it-yourself soul satisfaction regimen is much more pragmatic than it is praiseworthy. If I haven't laid up for myself "treasures on earth," it's because I already know they wouldn't be enough. I need more than an external facade of goodness. I need true, abiding righteousness. And I want more than an occasional reckless, sin-induced thrill. I long for a passionate, abundant life. I don't want my mistakes to be excused or overlooked—I ache for them to be forgiven and seen no more. I want unconditional love and a home for my wandering heart—but I want both of these to be permanent and irrevocable. I want the kind of great life that only a great God can give.

The longest chapter in the Gospel of John (chapter 6) renders a robust picture of the life-giving Jesus that I've come to love. First he feeds a multitude with five loaves and two fish; later in the same day he walks out on the turbulent sea to soothe his storm-rattled disciples, then the very waves themselves. He teaches the crowds who've followed him hoping to see another miraculous sign and asks them instead to recognize him for who he is: the Bread of Life. They grouse and grumble at his bothersome metaphor, saying, "How can this man be bread from heaven? We *know* him. He's from the neighborhood, for Pete's sake." They ask him for signs when they've already seen dozens. He asks them to believe because they've seen *him*.

Later, at a synagogue in Capernaum, his words take on an even more strange and terrible aspect: He speaks to his followers of eating his flesh and drinking his blood as a means to eternal life. They are horrified. (They liked the lunchtime loaves and fish program better.) Then John writes these words: "As a result of this many of His disciples withdrew and were not walking with Him anymore" (John 6:66).

Seeing them depart, Jesus said to the twelve men closest to him, "You do not want to go away also, do you?" (v. 67).

Simon Peter, typically more audacious than accurate, this one time gets it right: "Lord, to whom shall we go? You have the words of eternal life. We have believed and come to know that You are the Holy One of God" (v. 69).

Oh my. Peter had been hemmed in by the awesome power of the living Christ, and he surely knew it. No other teacher could touch his truth. No other friend was so winsome and wise. And no other prophet had eternity bred into his very bones and blood. Following him was sometimes confusing and even downright frightening. But having first believed, then come to know this Holy One of God, there was simply nowhere else for Peter to go.

Every great sinner needs a great God—one who will never relax or deny his own holiness to accommodate anything short of the repentance he requires. A God who will not release his child from discipline but who heals and bandages the loving wounds he makes. "In Him," Paul writes, "we have redemption through His blood, the forgiveness of our trespasses, according to the riches of His grace" (Eph. 1:7). The prophet Hosea, writing hundreds of years before Paul, sends his own ripple across the ageless river of mercy: "He has wounded us, but he will bandage us. He will revive us; . . . He will raise us up . . . that we may live before Him" (Hosea 6:1–2).

A great sinner needs a great God. And a dead spirit needs a living Savior.

There is only one place where an unresponsive heart can be made to quicken, and that is in the presence of the resurrected Christ. "Where else shall we go?" said Peter. What masquerades for life in this life is not life at all. He *himself* is the life. "But God, being rich in mercy, because of His great love with which He loved us, even when we were dead in our transgressions, made us alive together with Christ" (Eph. 2:4–5). Anyone who has known how it is to be a dead man walking can never forget who it was that revived him.

We are great sinners who need a great God, and we have dead hearts that need reviving. But maybe more than anything, we are lost souls who need to find our way home.

G. K. Chesterton wrote, "We have come to the wrong star. That is what makes life so splendid and so strange. The true happiness is that we *don't* fit. We come from somewhere else. We have lost our way."[2] Where does a wandering heart find its home? In the knowledge of the Holy One—the other, eternal, awesome, almighty God. "Whatever was to my profit," wrote Paul, "I now consider loss for the sake of Christ. What is more, I consider everything a loss compared to the surpassing greatness of knowing Christ my Lord. . . . I consider them rubbish, that I may gain Christ, and *be found in him*" (Phil. 3:7–9, italics mine).

This is who *we* are. This is what *we* want and need. But what of God? What does he desire? My Girl Scout heart is already leaping with answers! He wants me to be good. He wants me to love others. He wants me to serve him. To bring him honor and glory. To keep his commandments. He wants me to love him utterly and completely above all else.

I certainly can't argue against any of these things, but I can point to their ego-centeredness. More than God wants me to perform for him, he wants me to relax and lean into him, like John did as he laid his head on Jesus's chest one fateful night at dinner. God is, in fact, crystal clear about his druthers: "For I delight in loyalty rather than sacrifice," he said, "and in the knowledge of God rather than burnt offerings" (Hosea 6:6). He doesn't expect me to pirouette for him on the head of a pharisaical hat pin. He wants me to cling to him with a heart full of desire and to depend upon all that I have come to know of him like a hungry child depends on his mother for his next meal.

And why? Why does he want me to hold tightly to him and look only to him to fill me up? Because he means to feed me, and all those he loves, at a table in the wilderness.

The Edwards Plateau covers over twenty million acres in south central Texas with a limestone shield broken in places by eroded valleys, weathered hills, and steep outcroppings of ancient rock. Comanche Indians once lived there, but now it is mostly grazing country for sheep and goats and home to some of the state's most popular parks. A few miles out of Uvalde is a wild game ranch where I've spent some memorable hours on "retreat" with friends and co-workers, and while I can't in fairness label it true "wilderness," it is wilder than most places I frequent.

On one such trip, our host invited us on a hike to see a primitive cabin he'd built "up a ways" on a bluff, promising us a view that would make getting there well worth the effort (with emphasis on *getting there*, not on *effort*). Twenty or so of us started off in clumps of four or five, making our way first through gently sloping grasslands, then rockier terrain, and finally, after a half hour or so, to a more challenging climb than most of us expected.

I was in jeans and the kind of thin-soled tennis shoes that would have been better suited for cheerleading tryouts than rock-scaling, and every time I put my foot down, I prayed it would hold until I picked it up again. We laughed at our struggle, but it was the kind of laughter that's meant to cover serious concern. Up ahead on what merely pretended to be a trail, some of the early sprinters were perched on rocks, breathing hard and waiting for a second wind. No one seemed to know how far we had to go, but one look back quickly confirmed how far (and high) we'd come.

As for me, my calves ached, and sweat was stinging the corners of my eyes. I wanted to turn around and go back down, but I knew I had come too far to quit. Then, when we couldn't possibly feel any more lost, we heard voices we recognized above us, calling out words of encouragement. "You're almost here. Keep on coming. You're doing great." The impossible angle leveled out a bit, and, hauling ourselves up over the next ledge, we were in the clear.

Lou, the owner of the ranch, was crouched over an open fire, cooking venison sausage and buffalo steaks. There was a cooler with bottled water open for us, and a mesh bag of fresh, fragrant oranges was open on an old cedar wood table. I'd never been so satisfied by water, and I savored every sip.

As we breathed in the smell of burning mesquite and sizzling meat, we began to cool down and look around. Lou was right. The climb *was* worth the view. But if you had asked me just ten short minutes before, I would have sworn that it couldn't possibly be. All I had wanted then was to survive our little "hike" without sliding face-first down the side of a cliff, and now I was preparing to enjoy an unexpected meal that would taste better *because* of the climb, not in spite of it. When I couldn't see past my next foothold—all the while that I was climbing—someone was preparing for me a table in the wilderness.

We stayed "up top" for nearly an hour more, savoring the sound of the wind through the junipers and cedars and the giddy laughter of the recently threatened, then mercifully spared. My fingers were sticky with the juice from a peeled orange, and when I licked my lips, I could taste the salt of good, grilled meat. I was so tired, and full, and incredibly happy to be there, surrounded by the fierce beauty of that place and the people I loved.

I found a picture of us all a while back, gathered on the top of the rock, shoulder to shoulder, squinting into the afternoon sun. Kevin has gone to Washington state to start a home church from ground zero. Julie's a stay-at-home mom these days; her circle of influence is smaller but I suspect vastly deeper than before. Charlie's gone home to be with Jesus, and this is the only photograph I still have of him. Heaven is sweeter to me because he lives there. Keith is grinning just the other side of Charlie, and he's still serving faithfully where he's been for nearly ten years now. The photo also reminds me of Jane, although she's not even in it; at ninety, she didn't make the climb with us, and she's since gone home too. It was a good day, and it is almost as good in the remembering as it was in the tasting.

When do we lose that childhood love of what might be next? At what age or stage do we become so focused on conquering the immediate that we don't dare think of the imagined? Maybe we've so successfully rewired our hearts to tend to *doing* that we've forgotten what it's like to dream. I wonder how many of us actually remember so little of our God's great love that we think there's nothing more to look forward to. I know I am ashamed of how little it takes to satisfy me some days.

"We are half-hearted creatures," wrote C. S. Lewis, "fooling about with drink and sex and ambition when infinite joy is offered us, like an ignorant child who wants to go on making mud pies in a slum because he cannot imagine what is meant by the offer of a holiday at the sea. We are far too easily pleased."[3]

If we've given ourselves over to little more than duty and order and serviceable worship, it may be not because we don't believe anything more exists but because we don't believe it can be *ours*. We've stopped imagining that God could surprise us at any turn, take our breath away around the next bend, or cause our metronome-steady hearts to flutter out of time with some unexpected jolt of joy.

But he could, of course—and why wouldn't he? Why wouldn't the One who has already given his only Son to win us back offer random reminders of that bottomless love through the days of our lives that remain until we sit down together at another table—the one he's prepared for us not in the wilderness but in the wild new world we're destined for? And why shouldn't the wilderness whet our appetite with cool water and steak and oranges until we taste true delight at the marriage supper of the Lamb?

We are not there yet. This wide place we are traveling through is mean and harsh and most unwelcoming at times—but that is no reason to imagine it is not crammed with hints of the glory that will one day be ours. And while we hope for what we cannot see, there is more than enough room and reason to delight in what our eyes can already comprehend: the daily, fleeting glimpses of his goodness that are everywhere, always. We are made for just that kind of joy.

I was moaning to a friend that I was ready for all the difficulties I was experiencing to be over. I wanted to rest. I wanted to be assured of my safety. I wanted goodness to win out over evil and pain to disappear. "You want it to be over?" he asked. (I thought that was what I just said. Was he checking his own hearing?) "I do," I said emphatically.

*Then he let me have it: "You know when this part is over, Leigh?
It's over when you die. Are you ready for it to be over?" When he put
it that way, I wasn't. Not so much. It's not that I don't want to be with
Jesus. I do. But I love this place I'm journeying through. Even at its
wretched worst, it's richly seasoned with the glory of God, and I want
to taste still more of it.*

*Can you think of a time when God served up a little bit of heaven
to you in the very midst of your very worst? I hope you didn't sniff at
the spread and forgo the feast out of bitterness or weariness or fear. The
next time he spreads for you a table in the wilderness, deliberately sit
down. Make yourself comfortable. Consider it the delightful appetizer
for the endless years you'll spend in heaven's dining hall.*

"You prepare a table before me in the presence of
my enemies; You have anointed my head with oil; my
cup overflows. Surely goodness and lovingkindness
will follow me all the days of my life, and I will dwell
in the house of the LORD forever" (Ps. 23:5–6).

"Blessed are those who hunger and thirst for
righteousness, for they shall be satisfied" (Matt. 5:6).

"Jesus then said to them, 'Truly, truly, I say to you,
it is not Moses who has given you the bread out of
heaven, but it is My Father who gives you the true
bread out of heaven. For the bread of God is that
which comes down out of heaven, and gives life to the
world" (John 6:32–33).

"Our Father who is in heaven, hallowed be Your
name. Your kingdom come, Your will be done, on
earth as it is in heaven" (Matt. 6:9–10).

Epilogue

Filippo Lippi's *Predella of the Barbadori Altarpiece* hangs in the Uffizi in Florence, Italy. The painting depicts St. Augustine sitting at a desk that looks amazingly like a modern office cubicle. With a scroll on his knee and a pen in hand, Augustine gazes at a flaming visage of the Holy Trinity hovering just above his bookshelf—and pays no attention to the three long arrows that pierce his heart. His face bears no agony, no terror. Whatever pain he feels (and he must, for the arrows are not small) is a pain he sits still for, and maybe even loves.

Real life seldom fulfills our wildest hopes, and the gap between what we have and what we long for can open quite wide. Occasionally we catch a vision of truth and beauty that takes our breath away and reminds us of what we miss. We are richer if we do not look away.

"We are born to love as we are born to die, and between the heartbeats of these two great mysteries lies all the tangled undergrowth of our tiny lives. There is nowhere to go but through . . . in the mapless wilderness of love."[1]

Notes

Prologue

1. C. S. Lewis, *Mere Christianity* (New York: Macmillan, 1952), 105.

Chapter 4: One Golden Dancing Shoe

1. Derek Webb, "Dance," © 2000 Niphon, Inc. (admin. by Music Services). All rights reserved. ASCAP.

2. *Babette's Feast*, DVD, directed by Gabriel Axel (1987; Los Angeles, CA: MGM Home Entertainment, 2001).

3. Ibid.

4. Ibid.

Chapter 5: The Front Porch Castaway

1. William Bennett, *The Book of Virtues* (New York: Simon & Schuster, 1998), 493.

2. William Shakespeare, *Shakespeare's King Henry V*, Standard English Classics (Boston: Athenaeum Press, Ginn & Company, 1908), 105.

3. Ibid., 130.

4. Ibid., 130–31.

5. G. K. Chesterton, *Brave New Family*, ed. Alvaro De Silva (San Francisco: Ignatius Press, 1990), 52.

Chapter 6: "Have Courage"

1. Thomas Schmidt, *A Scandalous Beauty* (Grand Rapids: Brazos Press, 2002), 16.

2. Emily Dickinson, *Emily Dickinson, Selected Poems*, Bloomsbury Poetry Classics (New York: St. Martin's Press, 1992), 40.

3. Kenneth Branagh, *Beginning* (New York: W.W. Norton & Company, 1989), 22.

4. Ken Gire, *Windows of the Soul* (Grand Rapids: Zondervan, 1996), 218.

Chapter 7: One Bright Red Bird

1. Emily Dickinson, "Hope is the thing with feathers" in *Collected Poems of Emily Dickinson* (repr., New York: Gramercy Books, 1988).

2. Nancy Gibbs, "Making Time for a Baby," *Time*, April 15, 2002.

Chapter 8: Faith and Falling

1. Madeleine L'Engle, *The Weather of the Heart* (Wheaton: Harold Shaw, 1978), 45.

2. Brennan Manning, *Ruthless Trust* (San Francisco: HarperSanFrancisco, 2000), 7.

3. Alfred Edersheim, *The Life and Times of Jesus the Messiah* (Peabody, MA: Hendrikson, 1993), 846.

Chapter 9: "Gimme Some Sugar"

1. Emily Dickinson, "I shall know why—when Time is over" in *Collected Poems of Emily Dickinson* (repr., New York: Gramercy Books, 1988), 250.

2. John Piper, "Christ and Cancer" (sermon, August 17, 1980), available at http://www.desiringgod.org.

3. Ibid.

4. Eugene H. Peterson, *Subversive Spirituality* (Grand Rapids: Eerdmans, 1997), 165.

5. J. R. R. Tolkien, *The Return of the King* (Boston: Houghton Mifflin, 1983), 124.

6. Ibid., 136.

7. Ibid., 138–39.

8. Ibid., 144.

Chapter 11: New Clothes for Cara

1. "Letter of His Holiness Pope John Paul II to Artists," 4 April 1999, the Vatican.

2. Gerard Manley Hopkins, "Pied Beauty," in *Poems of Gerard Manley Hopkins* (London: Humphrey Milford, 1918), n. 13, www.bartleby.com/122.

Chapter 12: Old Addresses

1. Frederick Buechner, *A Room Called Remember* (San Francisco: HarperSanFrancisco, 1984), 4.

2. Ibid.

3. Oswald Chambers, *The Best from All His Books*, ed. Harry Verploegh (Nashville: Nelson Books, 1989), 14.

Chapter 13: "You're Fired!"

1. Dorothy L. Sayers, *Creed or Chaos?* (Manchester, NH: Sophia Institute Press, 1974), 73.

2. Ibid., 63, 73.

3. Alyson Footer, "Astros Outlast Braves, Head to NLCS," October 10, 2005, mlb.com.

4. Sayers, *Creed*, 73.

5. Irving Stone, ed., *Dear Theo; the Autobiography of Vincent van Gogh* (New York: Penguin Books, 1969), 103.

Chapter 14: Lost Causes

1. Not his real name.

Chapter 15: Goodbye, Rhett Butler

1. Peter Kreeft, *Love Is Stronger than Death* (San Francisco: Ignatius Press, 1979), 43.

2. Martin Luther, *Sermons of Martin Luther: The House Postils*, ed. Eugene Klug (Grand Rapids: Baker, 1996), 1:116.

3. Thornton Wilder, *Our Town* (New York: Coward-McCann, 1938; repr., Harper, 1957), 124–25, 127–28.

4. Kreeft, *Love Is Stronger*, 48–49.

Chapter 16: Singing the Hymnal

1. Chris Rice, "Hallelujahs," © 1995 Clumsy Fly Music (Admin. by Word Music, LLC). All rights reserved. Used by permission.

2. Fanny J. Crosby and John R. Sweney, "Tell Me the Story of Jesus," *Baptist Hymnal* (Nashville: Convention Press, 1956), 211.

3. Palmer Hartsough and James H. Fillmore, "I Am Resolved," *Baptist Hymnal* (Nashville: Convention Press, 1956), 216.

4. Fanny J. Crosby and George C. Stebbins, "Jesus Is Tenderly Calling," *Baptist Hymnal* (Nashville: Convention Press, 1956), 229.

5. Fanny J. Crosby and William H. Doane, "I Am Thine, O Lord," *Baptist Hymnal* (Nashville: Convention Press, 1956), 349.

6. Reginald Heber and John B. Dykes, "Holy, Holy, Holy," *Baptist Hymnal* (Nashville: Convention Press, 1956), 1.

7. Mary Byrne, "Be Thou My Vision," *Baptist Hymnal* (Nashville: Convention Press, 1956), 62.

8. Scotty Smith, *The Reign of Grace* (West Monroe, LA: Howard Publishers, 2003), 202.

9. Edward Perronet and William Shrubsole, "All Hail the Power of Jesus' Name," *Baptist Hymnal* (Nashville: Convention Press, 1956), 133.

Chapter 17: A Table in the Wilderness

1. Derek Webb, "Lover," © 2002 Derek Webb Music (admin. by Music Services). All rights reserved. ASCAP.

2. G. K. Chesterton, *Orthodoxy?* (Westport, CT: Greenwood, 1974).

3. C. S. Lewis, *The Weight of Glory and Other Addresses* (San Francisco: Harper-Collins, 2001), 26.

Epilogue

1. Tim Farrington, *The Monk Downstairs* (San Francisco: HarperSanFranciso, 2002), 261.

Leigh McLeroy writes and speaks with a passion for God and a keen eye for his presence in everyday life. A former ghostwriter with seven books to her credit, Leigh's first solo effort, *Moments for Singles*, was published in 2004. She was a contributor to Rebecca St. James's *Sister Freaks* in 2006, and is also a feature writer and the creator of *Wednesday words*, an email devotional with a life of its own. A frequent conference and event speaker, Leigh makes her home in Houston, Texas, where she is raising Owen—who may be the most adorable spaniel ever named after an Inkling, a John Irving character, *and* a Puritan preacher.

MORE *soul-stirring* BOOKS *from* REVELL

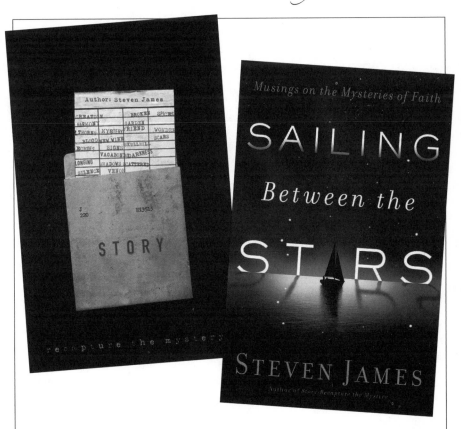

"A journey full of wonder, tears, joy, despair, and hope revealed through the eyes and heart of a storyteller."

—*Publishers Weekly*, starred review for *Story: Recapture the Mystery*